low fat
pasta

valerie ferguson

low fat
pasta

a tempting collection
of delicious recipes
that won't affect
your waistline

southwater

This edition is published by Southwater

Southwater is an imprint of
Anness Publishing Ltd
Hermes House
88–89 Blackfriars Road
London SE1 8HA
tel. 020 7401 2077
fax 020 7633 9499

Distributed in the USA by
Anness Publishing Inc.
27 West 20th Street
Suite 504
New York, NY 10011
fax 212 807 6813

Distributed in the UK by
The Manning Partnership
251–253 London Road East
Batheaston, Bath BA1 7RL
tel. 01225 852 727
fax 01225 852 852

Distributed in Australia by
Sandstone Publishing
Unit 1, 360 Norton Street, Leichhardt
New South Wales 2040
tel. 02 9560 7888
fax 02 9560 7488

A CIP catalogue record for this book is available from the British Library.

Publisher: Joanna Lorenz
Editor: Valerie Ferguson
Designer: Carole Perks
Typesetter: Diane Pullen
Editorial Reader: Richard McGinlay
Production Controller: Don Campaniello

Recipes contributed by:
Catherine Atkinson, Alex Barker, Michelle Berriedale-Johnson, Angela Boggiano, Janet Brinkworth,
Carla Capalbo, Kit Chan, Jacqueline Clark, Maxine Clarke, Frances Cleary, Trish Davies, Roz Denny,
Patrizia Diemling, Matthew Drennan, Sarah Edmonds, Rafi Fernandez, Christine France, Sarah Gates,
Shirley Gill, Nicola Graimes, Rosamund Grant, Rebekah Hassan, Deh-Ta Hsuing, Shehzad Husain,
Christine Ingram, Judy Jackson, Masaki Ko, Lesley Mackley, Norma MacMillan, Sue Maggs, Kathy Man,
Elizabeth Martin, Sallie Morris, Annie Nichols, Maggie Pannell, Katherine Richmond, Anne Sheasby,
Jenny Stacey, Liz Trigg, Hilaire Walden, Laura Washburn, Steven Wheeler, Judy Williams, Jeni Wright

Photography:
William Adams-Lingwood, Karl Adamson, Edward Allwright, David Armstrong, Steve Baxter, Micki Dowie,
James Duncan, John Freeman, Ian Garlick, Michelle Garrett, John Heseltine, Amanda Heywood,
Janine Hosegood, David Jordan, Don Last, Patrick McLeavey, Thomas Odulate, Juliet Piddington, Peter Reilly

Previously published as part of a larger compendium, *Pasta*

1 3 5 7 9 10 8 6 4 2

Contents

Introduction

Italians are passionate about food and always enjoy spending time preparing, cooking and eating meals with family and friends. Food is one of their greatest pleasures, and Italians are fortunate to be able to enjoy many regional variations in the dishes they eat. Pasta, a central part of Italian cuisine, is thought by many of us to be laden with calories and fat, but in fact it can be enjoyed as part of a healthy, low-fat diet.

Many traditional Italian ingredients, such as the abundance of fresh Mediterranean sun-ripened vegetables, fresh herbs and numerous different types of pasta, are naturally low in fat,

making them ideal to enjoy as part of a low-fat eating plan. Quality and freshness of foods are both of great importance to the Italians, and much of the fresh produce eaten is grown or produced locally. When it comes to cooking ingredients such as vegetables, they are often prepared in simple ways to bring out their delicious and natural flavors.

Olive oil is the primary fat used for cooking in Italy, and it is also commonly used for dressing foods such as salads. Olive oil is a "healthier" type of fat that is high in monounsaturated fat and low in saturated fat, and as long as it is used in moderation, it can also be enjoyed as part of a low-fat diet.

Some other typical Italian ingredients, such as pancetta, salami, Parmesan and mozzarella, are high in fat but are easily substituted with lower-fat foods such as lean bacon and reduced-fat mozzarella or, in many recipes, the amount of the high-fat food can often simply be reduced to lower the fat content of the dish.

In Italy, pasta dishes form a large part of the cuisine, and the many varieties are ideal for a low-fat diet, as they are naturally high in carbohydrates and low in fat, as long as the sauce served with the pasta dish is also low in fat!

Most of us eat fats in some form or another every day, and we all need a small amount of fat in our diet to maintain a healthy, balanced eating plan. However, most of us eat far too much fat, and we should all be looking to reduce our overall fat intake, especially saturated fats.

Ounce for ounce, dietary fats supply much more energy than all the other nutrients in our diet, and if you eat a diet that is high in fat but don't exercise enough to use up that energy, you will gain weight.

By cutting down on the amount of fat you eat and making easy changes to your diet, such as choosing the right types of fat, using low-fat and fat-free products whenever possible and making simple changes to the way you prepare

and cook food, you will soon be reducing your overall fat intake and enjoying a much healthier lifestyle—and you'll hardly notice the difference!

As you will see from this cookbook, it is certainly easy to eat and enjoy pasta dishes as part of a low-fat eating plan. We have included some Asian noodle dishes as they offer variety and a distinctly different flavor, while still being low in fat. We provide lots of useful and informative advice, including an introduction to basic healthy eating guidelines, helpful hints and tips on low-fat and fat-free ingredients and low-fat and fat-free cooking techniques, and practical tips on how to reduce fat and saturated fat in your diet.

All the recipes in this cookbook are very low in fat—each contains 15 grams of fat or less per serving; some contain less than 5 grams of fat per serving.

You will be surprised and delighted by this tempting collection of recipes, which range from soups and salads to main-course pasta and noodle dishes, with fish and shellfish, poultry, meat and vegetables. All the recipes contain less fat than similar recipes, and yet they are packed full of flavor. This inspirational cookbook, with over 140 mouthwatering recipes, will give you valuable insight into low-fat cooking, and will enable you to enjoy food that is healthy, delicious and nutritious, as well as low in fat.

Fat & Calorie Counter

The following figures show the weight of fat (g) and the energy content per 3½ ounces.

Vegetables	Fat (g)	Energy
Artichokes, globe, boiled	0.2	24 Cals
Asparagus, boiled	0.6	25 Cals
Bell Peppers, red, raw	0.4	32 Cals
Broccoli, raw	0.9	33 Cals
Carrots, raw	0.9	35 Cals
Celery, raw	0.2	7 Cals
Corn, canned	1.1	110 Cals
Eggplant, raw	0.4	15 Cals
Fennel, Florence, raw	0.2	12 Cals
Mushrooms, raw	0.4	13 Cals
Olives, in brine	11.0	103 Cals
Onions, raw	0.2	36 Cals
Peas, raw	1.5	83 Cals
Spinach, raw	0.8	25 Cals
Tomatoes, raw	0.3	17 Cals
Zucchini, raw	0.4	18 Cals

Fruit, Nuts & Seeds		
Apples, raw	0.1	47 Cals
Oranges	0.1	37 Cals
Peanuts	13.3	150 Cals
Pine nuts	68.6	688 Cals
Walnuts	68.5	688 Cals

Pasta & Noodles		
Egg noodles, boiled	0.4	56 Cals
Pasta, white, cooked	0.7	104 Cals
Pasta, whole-wheat, cooked	0.9	113 Cals

Cereals, Beans & Pulses		
Bread, white	1.9	235 Cals
Chickpeas	0.7	29 Cals
Flour, all-purpose	1.2	307 Cals
Green and brown lentils, cooked	0.7	105 Cals
Red kidney beans, canned	0.6	100 Cals
Sesame seeds	145	150 Cals
Soy sauce	0.0	11 Cals
Tofu/beancurd	3.8	63 Cals

Fish & Shellfish		
Anchovies, canned in oil	19.9	280 Cals
Clams, canned in natural juice	0.6	77 Cals
Crab, canned in brine	0.5	77 Cals
Salmon, raw	11.0	180 Cals
Salmon, smoked	4.5	142 Cals
Salmon, steamed	11.9	194 Cals
Scallops, steamed	1.4	118 Cals
Shrimp, boiled	0.9	99 Cals
Squid, raw	1.7	81 Cals
Trout, cooked	1.4	34 Cals
Tuna, canned in water	0.6	99 Cals

Meat & Poultry		
Bacon, lean, broiled	5.2	172 Cals
Beef, ground, extra lean, stewed	6.6	121 Cals
Beef, topside, lean, roast	4.4	156 Cals
Chicken breast, no skin, roast	1.1	153 Cals
Chicken livers, fried	8.0	152 Cals
Duck, meat only, roast	10.4	195 Cals
Lamb, leg, lean, roast	9.6	210 Cals
Pork, leg, lean, roast	6.9	185 Cals
Sausage, reduced-fat, broiled	12.4	207 Cals
Turkey, meat only, roast	2.0	153 Cals

Dairy Products, Fats & Oils		
Butter	81.7	737 Cals
Cottage cheese	11.7	173 Cals
Cream cheese	47.4	439 Cals
Eggs, whole, raw	10.8	147 Cals
Egg white, raw	Trace	36 Cals
Egg yolk, raw	30.5	339 Cals
Fromage frais, plain	7.1	113 Cals
Fromage frais, very low-fat	0.2	58 Cals
Low-fat cottage cheese	1.4	78 Cals
Low-fat crème fraîche	15.0	165 Cals
Low-fat cream cheese	Trace	74 Cals
Low-fat spread	40.5	390 Cals
Low-fat yogurt	0.8	56 Cals
Milk, skim	0.1	33 Cals
Olive oil	99.9	899 Cals
Parmesan cheese	32.7	452 Cals
Peanut/Vegetable/Sesame oil	89.9	809 Cals
Ricotta cheese	11.0	144 Cals
Very low-fat spread	25.0	273 Cals

Alcohol & Sugar		
Red wine	0.0	17 Cals
White wine	0.0	17 Cals
White sugar	0.0	355 Cals

Information from *The Composition of Foods* (5th Edition, 1991) is Crown copyright and is reproduced with the permission of the Royal Society of Chemistry and the Controller of Her Majesty's Stationery Office.

Types of Pasta

There are at least 200 different types of pasta—and there can sometimes seem to be about ten times as many names.

Most pasta is made from durum wheat flour, which is quite hard and does not get soggy when cooked. Dried pasta may simply have been mixed with water or may also contain egg, while fresh pasta— *pasta all'uova*—always contains egg. As a result of a growing interest in healthy foods, whole-wheat pasta, which has a rich brown color, has become increasingly popular. Buckwheat pasta, which is an even darker color, is also available and is suitable for people on a gluten-free diet. Pasta may be colored and flavored with a range of ingredients. The most common additions are tomatoes and spinach, but beets, saffron, herbs, wild mushrooms and cuttlefish ink are also widely used. There are no hard-and-fast rules about which shapes to serve with particular sauces, but some shapes do work better than others. The recipes in this book include one or more recommendations, but you can substitute a shape of your choice.

Hollow Pasta
These include penne, fusilli, macaroni, farfalle, rigatoni, orecchiette, rotelli, tortiglioni, chifferi rigati, ruote and mezze. Try these with robust sauces, such as cheese, tomato and vegetable.

Long Pasta
These include spaghetti, linguine, tagliatelle, tagliarini and fettuccine. Some are flat ribbons, while others are hollow tubes. All go well with smooth and creamy sauces and vegetable sauces with finely chopped ingredients.

Filled Pasta
These include ravioli, cappelletti and tortelloni. These are good with simple sauces, such as tomato.

Pasta for Baking
These include very delicate shapes, such as risi and orzi, as well as larger ones for more robust dishes—tubetti, conchiglie, cannelloni and lasagne, for example.

Above: A selection of the many different types of pasta.

Basic Pasta Dough
Serves 3–4
1¾ cups all-purpose flour, (Italian tipo 00 is the best if you can find it)
pinch of salt
2 eggs
2 teaspoons cold water

Variations:
Tomato: add 4 teaspoons concentrated tomato paste to the eggs before mixing.
Spinach: add 4 ounces frozen spinach, thawed and squeezed of excess moisture. Combine or process with the eggs, before adding the mixture to the flour.
Herb: add 3 tablespoons finely chopped fresh herbs to the eggs before mixing the dough.
Whole-wheat: use 2 ounces all-purpose flour and 5 ounces whole-wheat flour. Add an extra 2 teaspoons cold water.

Making Pasta by Hand

1 Sift the flour and salt onto a clean work surface and make a well in the center with your hand.

2 Put the eggs and water into the well. Using a fork, beat the eggs gently together, then gradually draw in the flour from the sides, combining to make a thick pasta.

3 When the mixture becomes too stiff to use a fork, use your hands to continue to combine to form a firm dough. Knead the dough for about 5 minutes, until it is smooth.

4 Wrap the dough in plastic wrap and let it rest for 20–30 minutes.

SOUPS & SALADS

Puglia-style Minestrone

Ricotta salata is the traditional garnish for this simple soup. You don't need to use much; even a small sprinkling boosts the flavor.

Serves 4
2 skinless, boneless chicken thighs
1 onion, quartered lengthwise
1 carrot, roughly chopped
1 celery stalk, roughly chopped
a few black peppercorns
1 small handful mixed fresh
   herbs, such as parsley
   and thyme
1 chicken bouillon
5 cups water
1/2 cup dried tubetti
salt and freshly ground
   black pepper
1 ounce ricotta salata, coarsely
   grated or crumbled and
   2 tablespoons fresh mint
   leaves, to serve

1 Put the chicken thighs in a large saucepan. Add the onion, carrot, celery, peppercorns and herbs, then crumble in the bouillon cube. Pour in the water and bring to a boil.

2 Lower the heat, half cover the pan and simmer gently for about 1 hour. Remove the pan from heat. Let the liquid cool, then strain it into a clean large saucepan. Discard the flavoring ingredients. Blot the surface with paper towels to remove surface fat.

3 Cut the chicken into bite-size pieces and set aside.

4 Bring the stock in the pan to a boil, add the pasta and simmer, stirring until only just al dente.

5 Add the pieces of chicken and heat through for a few minutes. Taste for seasoning. Serve hot in warmed bowls, sprinkled with the ricotta salata and mint leaves.

Cook's Tip
Ricotta salata is a salted and dried version of ricotta, which can easily be crumbled. If it is not available, crumbled feta cheese can be used instead.

Pasta Soup with Chicken Livers

A soup that can be served as either a first or main course. The fried chicken livers are so delicious that even if you do not normally like them, you will relish them in this soup.

Serves 4–6
2/3 cup chicken livers, thawed
   if frozen
3 sprigs each fresh parsley,
   marjoram and sage
leaves from 1 fresh thyme sprig
5–6 fresh basil leaves
1 tablespoon olive oil
4 garlic cloves, crushed
1–2 tablespoons dry
   white wine
2 11-ounce cans condensed
   chicken consommé
2 cups frozen peas
1/2 cup dried farfalle
2–3 scallions, sliced diagonally
salt and freshly ground
   black pepper

1 Cut the chicken livers into small pieces with scissors. Finely chop the herbs. Heat the olive oil in a frying pan, add the garlic and herbs, season with salt and pepper to taste, and sauté gently for a few minutes.

2 Add the chicken livers, increase the heat to high and stir-fry for a few minutes, until they change color and become dry. Pour in the wine, cook until it evaporates, then remove the livers from heat and taste for seasoning.

3 Pour both cans of condensed chicken consommé into a large saucepan and add water to the condensed soup as directed on the labels. Add an extra can of water, then stir in a little salt and pepper to taste and bring to a boil.

4 Add the frozen peas to the pan and simmer for about 5 minutes, then add the pasta and bring the soup back to a boil, stirring. Let simmer, stirring frequently, until the pasta is only just al dente.

5 Add the fried chicken livers and scallions, and heat through for 2–3 minutes. Taste for seasoning. Serve hot, in warmed bowls.

Broccoli, Anchovy & Pasta Soup

In this tasty soup, broccoli and anchovies make excellent partners for pretty little orecchiette.

Serves 4
2 tablespoons olive oil
1 small onion, finely chopped
1 garlic clove, finely chopped
1/4–1/3 fresh red chile, seeded and finely chopped
2 drained canned anchovies
scant 1 cup passata
3 tablespoons dry white wine
5 cups vegetable stock
2 cups broccoli florets
1¾ cups dried orecchiette
salt and freshly ground black pepper
freshly grated Pecorino cheese, to serve

1 Heat the olive oil in a large, heavy saucepan. Add the onion, garlic, chile and anchovies and cook over low heat, stirring constantly, for 5–6 minutes.

2 Add the passata and wine, and season with salt and pepper to taste. Bring to a boil, cover the pan, then cook over low heat, stirring occasionally, for 12–15 minutes.

3 Pour in the stock. Bring to a boil, then add the broccoli florets and simmer for about 5 minutes. Add the pasta and bring back to a boil, stirring.

4 Lower the heat and simmer, stirring frequently, until the pasta is al dente. Taste for seasoning and adjust, if necessary. Serve the soup hot, in warmed bowls, and pass the grated Pecorino cheese separately.

Cook's Tip
Salted dried anchovies have a better flavor and texture than canned anchovies, but are not so widely available. If using them, rinse thoroughly in cold water and pat dry on paper towels first. If they are still too salty, then soak them in milk for about 30 minutes, rinse in cold water and pat dry.

Clam & Pasta Soup

This soup is based on the classic pasta dish—spaghetti alle vongole—but uses staple ingredients. Serve it with hot focaccia or ciabatta for an informal dinner with friends.

Serves 4
2 tablespoons olive oil
1 large onion, finely chopped
2 garlic cloves, crushed
14-ounce can chopped tomatoes
1 tablespoon sun-dried tomato paste
1 teaspoon sugar
1 teaspoon mixed dried herbs
about 3 cups fish or vegetable stock
2/3 cup red wine
1/2 cup small dried pasta shapes
5-ounce jar or can clams in natural juice
2 tablespoons finely chopped fresh flat-leaf parsley, plus a few whole leaves, to garnish
salt and freshly ground black pepper

1 Heat the oil in a large saucepan. Cook the onion gently, stirring frequently, for 5 minutes, until softened.

2 Add the garlic, tomatoes, sun-dried tomato pureé, sugar, herbs, stock and wine, and season with salt and pepper to taste. Bring to a boil. Lower the heat, half cover the pan and simmer for 10 minutes, stirring occasionally.

3 Add the pasta and continue simmering, uncovered, until al dente. Stir occasionally, to prevent the pasta shapes from sticking together.

4 Add the clams and their juice to the soup and heat through for 3–4 minutes, adding more stock if needed. Do not let the soup boil or the clams will be tough.

5 Remove from heat, stir in the parsley and taste the soup for seasoning. Serve hot, sprinkled with coarsely ground black pepper and parsley leaves.

Corn Chowder with Conchigliette

Chowders are always wonderfully satisfying, and this one is no exception. It is low in fat, but high on the flavor stakes.

Serves 6–8
1 small green bell pepper, diced
1 pound potatoes, peeled
  and diced
2 cups drained canned or
  frozen corn
1 onion, chopped
1 celery stalk, chopped

bouquet garni (bay leaf, parsley
  stems and thyme)
2½ cups chicken stock
1¼ cups skim milk
½ cup dried conchigliette
5 ounces smoked turkey
  bacon, diced
salt and freshly ground
  black pepper
breadsticks, to serve

1 Put the diced green pepper in a bowl and pour in the boiling water to cover. Let stand for 2 minutes. Drain, rinse and drain again.

2 Put the green pepper into a large, heavy saucepan and add the potatoes, corn, onion, celery, bouquet garni and stock. Bring to a boil, lower the heat, cover and simmer for 20 minutes, until tender.

3 Add the milk, then season with salt and pepper to taste. Process half of the soup in a food processor or blender and return it to the pan. Add the conchigliette and simmer over low heat until the pasta is *al dente*.

4 Meanwhile, fry the diced turkey bacon quickly in a nonstick frying pan for 2–3 minutes. Stir them into the soup. Serve in warmed bowls, with breadsticks.

Pasta & Lentil Soup

Small brown lentils are partnered with pasta shapes in this wholesome soup, which is delicately flavored with fresh herbs.

Serves 4–6
1 cup brown lentils
2 tablespoons olive oil
2 strips bacon, diced
1 onion, finely chopped
1 celery stalk, finely chopped
1 carrot, finely chopped

8 cups chicken stock or water,
  or a combination
1 fresh sage leaf or a pinch of
  dried sage
1 fresh thyme sprig or
  ¼ teaspoon dried thyme
1½ cups ditalini or other small
  soup pasta
salt and freshly ground
  black pepper
flat-leaf parsley, to garnish

1 Pick over the lentils and remove any debris, such as small stones. Place the lentils in a bowl, pour in cold water to cover, and soak for 2–3 hours. Drain, rinse under cold running water and drain well again.

2 Heat the oil in a large saucepan and cook the bacon for 2–3 minutes. Add the onion, and cook gently until it softens.

3 Stir in the celery and carrot, and cook for 5 more minutes, stirring frequently. Add the lentils, stirring well.

4 Pour in the stock or water and the herbs, then bring the soup to a boil. Cook over medium heat for about 1 hour or until the lentils are tender. Add salt and pepper to taste.

5 Stir in the pasta, and cook until it is *al dente*. Let the soup stand for a few minutes before serving garnished with parsley.

Cook's Tip
If you use young organic vegetables, their flavor will probably be intense enough to make the addition of stock unnecessary. Just use water.

Chicken Noodle Soup

Just like Grandma used to make, this is comfort food, pure and simple.

Serves 8
1 chicken, about 3 pounds, cut into pieces
2 onions, quartered
1 parsnip, quartered
2 carrots, quartered
½ teaspoon salt
1 bay leaf
2 allspice berries
4 black peppercorns
6 cups water
4 ounces very thin egg noodles
fresh dill sprigs, to garnish

1 Put the chicken pieces, onions, parsnip, carrots, salt, bay leaf, allspice berries and peppercorns in a large saucepan.

2 Add the measured water. Bring to a boil, skimming the surface frequently, then lower the heat and simmer for about 1½ hours, skimming occasionally.

3 Strain the stock into a large bowl. Discard the vegetables and flavorings in the strainer, but remove the chicken pieces and set them aside.

4 When the chicken pieces are cool enough to handle, skin them and chop the flesh into bite-size pieces. Put these in a bowl. When both the chicken and the stock are cold, cover both the bowls and put them in the refrigerator overnight.

5 Next day, remove the solidified fat from the surface of the chilled stock. Pour it into a saucepan and bring to a boil.

6 Add the chicken and noodles, and cook until the noodles are *al dente*. Serve in warmed bowls, garnished with dill sprigs.

Cook's Tip
If you don't have time to chill the chicken stock in the refrigerator overnight, just blot the surface several times with paper towels to remove the excess fat.

Cock-a-Noodle Soup

Take a tasty trip to the Far East, with this quick and easy Chinese-style soup.

Serves 4–6
1 tablespoon corn oil
4 scallions, roughly chopped
8 ounces skinless, boneless chicken breasts, cut into small cubes
5 cups chicken stock
1 tablespoon soy sauce
1 cup frozen corn
4 ounces medium egg noodles
salt and freshly ground black pepper
1 carrot, thinly sliced lengthwise, to garnish

1 Heat the oil in a saucepan and sauté the scallions and chicken until the meat is evenly browned.

2 Add the stock and the soy sauce and bring to a boil, then stir in the corn.

3 Add the noodles, breaking them up roughly. Taste the soup and add salt and pepper if needed.

4 Use small cutters to stamp out shapes from the thin slices of carrot. Add them to the soup. Simmer for 5 minutes. Serve in warmed bowls.

Summer Minestrone

This brightly colored, fresh-tasting soup makes the most of summer vegetables. Peperini are very tiny, but you could use larger pasta shapes, if preferred.

Serves 4
1 tablespoon olive oil
1 large onion, finely chopped
1 tablespoon tomato paste
1 pound ripe Italian plum tomatoes, peeled and finely chopped
8 ounces zucchini, trimmed and roughly chopped
8 ounces yellow summer squash, trimmed and roughly chopped
3 waxy new potatoes, diced
2 garlic cloves, crushed
about 5 cups light chicken stock or water
¼ cup peperini
¼ cup shredded fresh basil
salt and freshly ground black pepper
grated Parmesan cheese, to serve (optional)

1 Heat the oil in a large saucepan. Add the onion and cook over low heat, stirring constantly, for about 5 minutes, until softened. Stir in the tomato paste, chopped tomatoes, zucchini, summer squash, diced potatoes and garlic. Mix well and cook gently for 10 minutes, uncovered, shaking the pan frequently to stop the vegetables from sticking to the bottom.

2 Pour in the stock or water and bring to a boil. Add the peperini, lower the heat, half cover the pan and simmer gently for 10–15 minutes or until both the vegetables and the pasta are just tender. Add more stock if necessary.

3 Remove the pan from heat and stir in the basil. Taste for seasoning and adjust, if necessary. Serve hot, sprinkled with a little Parmesan, if desired.

Chicken Vermicelli Soup with Egg Shreds

This soup is quick and easy to make, and very versatile. Add extra ingredients if desired, such as scallions, mushrooms, shrimp or chopped salami.

Serves 4–6

3 large eggs
2 tablespoons chopped cilantro
 or parsley
6 cups chicken stock
1 cup dried vermicelli or
 capelli d'angelo, broken into
 short lengths
4 ounces cooked chicken
 breast, shredded
salt and freshly ground
 black pepper

1 First, make the egg shreds. Whisk the eggs together in a small bowl and stir in the cilantro or parsley.

2 Heat a small nonstick frying pan and pour in about 3 tablespoons of the egg mixture, swirling to cover the bottom, and make a thin pancake. Cook until just set. Slide the pancake onto a plate and repeat until all the mixture is used up.

3 Roll each pancake up and, using a sharp knife, slice thinly crosswise into shreds. Set aside.

4 Bring the stock to a boil and add the pasta. Cook until it is almost *al dente*, then add the chicken and season with salt and pepper to taste. Heat through for 2–3 minutes, then stir in the egg shreds. Serve immediately.

Variation
To make a Thai variation, use Chinese rice noodles instead of vermicelli. Stir ½ teaspoon dried lemongrass, two small whole fresh green chiles and ¼ cup coconut milk into the chicken stock. Add four thinly sliced scallions and plenty of chopped cilantro.

Chicken & Stellette Soup

Little pasta stars look very attractive in this tasty soup, which is sophisticated enough to serve at a dinner party, yet has plenty of child appeal if you omit the wine.

4 ounces cooked, skinless chicken
 breast, thinly sliced
⅔ cup dry white wine
1 tablespoon chopped
 fresh parsley
salt and freshly ground
 black pepper

Serves 4–6

3¾ cups chicken stock
1 bay leaf
4 scallions, sliced
3 cups button mushrooms, sliced
½ cup stellette

1 Put the stock and bay leaf into a pan and bring to a boil over medium heat.

2 Add the scallions, mushrooms and pasta. Lower the heat, cover and simmer for 7–8 minutes.

3 Just before serving, add the chicken, wine and parsley, and season to taste. Heat through for 2–3 minutes, then serve in warmed bowls.

Variations
Any small soup pasta can be substituted for stellette— old-fashioned alphabet shapes are very popular with young children and will amuse nostalgic adults. "Safari" pasta is also fun. Let sit out the wine when making the soup for youngsters, and add a little extra stock instead.

Tiny Pasta in Broth

Serve this quick and easy soup with warm rolls for an after-theater dinner, or as a light appetizer before a hearty main course.

Serves 4

5 cups beef stock

³⁄₄ cup dried funghetti or other tiny soup pasta

2 pieces drained, bottled, roasted red bell pepper

salt and freshly ground black pepper

To serve

coarsely shaved Parmesan cheese (optional)

warm rolls

1 Bring the beef stock to a boil in a large saucepan. Season with salt and pepper to taste, then drop in the dried pasta. Stir well and bring the stock back to a boil.

2 Lower the heat to a simmer and cook until the pasta is *al dente*. Stir frequently.

3 Finely dice the pieces of roasted pepper. Divide them equally among four warmed soup plates. Taste the soup for seasoning and adjust, if necessary. Ladle into the soup plates and serve immediately, with shavings of Parmesan passed separately, if using, and a basket of warm rolls.

Cook's Tip

Bouillon are not really suitable for a recipe like this in which the flavor of the broth is important. If you don't have enough time to make your own stock, use two 11-ounce cans of good-quality condensed beef consommé, adding water as instructed on the labels.

Meatball & Pasta Soup

You can make a meal of this great soup, and it is very popular with children.

Serves 4

2 11-ounce cans condensed beef consommé

3¹⁄₂ ounces dried fedelini or spaghettini

fresh flat-leaf parsley to garnish

freshly grated Parmesan cheese, to serve (optional)

For the meatballs

1 very thick slice of white bread, crusts removed

2 tablespoons milk

8 ounces ground beef

1 garlic clove, crushed

1 tablespoon freshly grated Parmesan cheese

2–3 tablespoons fresh flat-leaf parsley leaves, coarsely chopped

1 egg

nutmeg

salt and freshly ground black pepper

1 First, make the meatballs. Break the bread into a small bowl, add the milk and set aside to soak. Meanwhile, put the beef, garlic, Parmesan, parsley and egg in another large bowl. Grate fresh nutmeg liberally on top and add salt and pepper to taste.

2 Squeeze the bread with your hands to remove as much milk as possible, then add the bread to the meatball mixture and combine well with your hands. Wash your hands, rinse them under cold water, then form the mixture into tiny balls about the size of small marbles.

3 Pour both cans of consommé into a large saucepan, add water as directed on the labels, then add an extra can of water. Stir in salt and pepper to taste and bring to a boil.

4 Drop in the meatballs, then break the pasta into small pieces and add it to the soup. Bring to a boil, stirring gently. Lower the heat and simmer, stirring frequently, until the pasta is *al dente*. Taste for seasoning and adjust, if necessary. Serve hot in warmed soup bowls, sprinkled with the parsley and freshly grated Parmesan cheese, if using.

Roasted Tomato & Pasta Soup

Roasting tomatoes really brings out their flavor, and the soup has a wonderful smoky taste.

Serves 4

1 pound ripe Italian plum
   tomatoes, halved lengthwise
1 large red bell pepper, quartered
   lengthwise and seeded
1 large red onion,
   quartered lengthwise
2 whole garlic cloves, unpeeled
1 tablespoon olive oil
5 cups vegetable stock or water
good pinch of sugar
scant 1 cup dried tubetti
   or other small pasta shapes
salt and freshly ground
   black pepper
fresh basil leaves, to garnish

1 Preheat the oven to 375°F. Spread out the tomatoes, red pepper, onion and unpeeled garlic cloves in a roasting pan. Drizzle with the olive oil. Roast for 30–40 minutes, until the vegetables are soft and charred, stirring and turning them halfway through the cooking time.

2 Transfer the vegetables to a food processor, add about 1 cup of the stock or water and process until puréed. Scrape into a sieve placed over a large saucepan and press the purée through into the pan.

3 Add the remaining stock or water, and the sugar, and season with salt and pepper to taste. Bring to a boil over medium heat, stirring constantly.

4 Add the pasta and cook, stirring frequently, until it is *al dente*. Taste for seasoning. Serve hot in warmed bowls, garnished with the fresh basil leaves.

> **Cook's Tip**
> *The soup can be frozen without the pasta. Thaw it thoroughly, pour it into a pan and bring it to a boil before adding the pasta.*

Farmhouse Soup

Rutabagas and turnips are often forgotten by modern cooks, which is a shame, for they have excellent flavor. Try them in this chunky, rustic main-course soup.

Serves 4

2 tablespoons olive oil
1 onion, roughly chopped
3 carrots, cut into large chunks
1 turnip, about 7 ounces, cut into
   large chunks
about 6 ounces rutabaga, cut into
   large chunks
14-ounce can chopped
   Italian tomatoes
1 tablespoon tomato paste
1 teaspoon mixed dried herbs
1 teaspoon dried oregano
½ cup dried bell peppers, washed
   and thinly sliced (optional)
6 cups vegetable stock or water
½ cup dried conchiglie or other
   pasta shapes
14-ounce can red kidney beans,
   rinsed and drained
2 tablespoons chopped fresh
   flat-leaf parsley
salt and freshly ground
   black pepper
freshly grated Parmesan
   cheese (optional) and crusty
   bread, to serve

1 Heat the olive oil in a large, heavy saucepan, add the onion and cook over low heat, stirring occasionally, for about 5 minutes, until softened.

2 Add the carrots, turnip, rutabaga, canned tomatoes, tomato paste, dried mixed herbs, oregano and dried peppers, if using. Season with salt and pepper to taste. Pour in the stock or water and bring to a boil over medium heat. Stir well, cover, lower the heat and simmer, stirring occasionally, for 30 minutes, until the vegetables are tender.

3 Add the pasta and bring to a boil, stirring constantly. Lower the heat and simmer until the pasta is only just *al dente*.

4 Stir in the kidney beans. Heat through for 2–3 minutes, then stir in the parsley. Serve hot in warmed soup bowls, with Parmesan passed separately, if using, and thick slices of crusty bread.

> **Cook's Tip**
> *Packages of dried Italian peppers are sold at many supermarkets. They are piquant and firm with a "meaty" bite to them, which makes them ideal for adding substance and concentrated flavor to soups.*

> **Variation**
> *Use two leeks instead of the onion and borlotti beans instead of the kidney beans. Virtually any small pasta shapes are suitable; chunky ones, such as pipe rigate or penne rigate, work best.*

Minestrone with Pasta & Beans

This tasty soup is made using canned beans, so is ideal for a spur-of-the-moment lunch invitation. A small amount of pancetta gives depth to the flavor.

Serves 4

1 tablespoon olive oil
2 ounces pancetta, rind removed, roughly chopped
2–3 celery stalks, finely chopped
3 carrots, finely chopped
1 onion, finely chopped
1–2 garlic cloves, crushed
2 14-ounce cans chopped tomatoes
about 4 cups chicken stock
14-ounce can cannellini beans, drained and rinsed
$\frac{1}{2}$ cup short-cut macaroni
2–4 tablespoons chopped flat-leaf parsley, to taste
salt and freshly ground black pepper
shaved Parmesan cheese, to serve (optional)

1 Heat the olive oil in a large, heavy saucepan. Add the pancetta, celery, carrots and onion, and cook over low heat for 5 minutes, stirring constantly, until the vegetables have begun to soften.

2 Add the garlic and tomatoes, breaking the tomatoes up well with a wooden spoon. Pour in the chicken stock. Season with salt and pepper to taste and bring to a boil. Half cover the pan, lower the heat and simmer gently for about 20 minutes, until the vegetables are soft.

3 Add the cannellini beans to the pan, together with the macaroni. Bring to a boil again. Cover, lower the heat and continue to simmer for about 20 minutes more, until the pasta is *al dente*.

4 Check the consistency of the soup and add a little more stock, if necessary. Stir in the parsley. Taste and adjust the seasoning, if necessary.

5 Serve hot in warmed soup bowls, sprinkling each portion with a few shavings of Parmesan cheese, if using.

Clear Vegetable Soup

The success of this clear soup depends on the quality of the stock, so it is best to use homemade vegetable stock, if possible, rather than bouillon cubes. Otherwise, you could use good-quality canned bouillon.

Serves 4

1 small carrot
1 baby leek
1 celery stalk
2 ounces green cabbage
$3\frac{3}{4}$ cups vegetable stock
1 bay leaf
1 cup drained cooked cannellini beans
$\frac{1}{4}$ cup dried soup pasta, such as tiny shells, bows, stars or elbows
salt and freshly ground black pepper
snipped fresh chives, to garnish

1 Cut the carrot, leek and celery into 2-inch long strips. Slice the cabbage very finely.

2 Put the stock and bay leaf into a large, heavy saucepan and bring to a boil over medium heat. Add the strips of carrot, leek and celery, lower the heat, cover the pan and simmer for 6 minutes.

3 Add the cabbage, cannellini beans and pasta shapes. Stir well to mix, then simmer, uncovered, for another 4–5 minutes or until all the vegetables are tender and the pasta is *al dente*.

4 Remove and discard the bay leaf, and season the soup to taste with salt and pepper. Ladle into four warmed soup bowls and garnish with the snipped chives. Serve immediately.

Variations
Use drained and rinsed canned cannellini beans to save time, if desired. Other beans that would also go well in this soup include flageolets, borlotti or navy. You could also substitute a shallot for the leek.

Navy Bean Soup with Pasta Shells

Soup you can almost stand a spoon in—that's what you get when you make this wonderful winter recipe.

Serves 6

1½ cups dried navy beans, soaked overnight in cold water to cover
7 cups unsalted vegetable stock or water
1 cup dried medium pasta shells
¼ cup olive oil, plus extra to serve
2 garlic cloves, crushed
¼ cup chopped fresh parsley
salt and freshly ground black pepper

1 Drain the beans and place them in a large saucepan. Add the stock or water. Bring to a boil, then lower the heat and simmer, half-covered, for 2–2½ hours or until tender.

2 Scoop half the beans and a little of their cooking liquid into a blender or food processor. Process into a purée, then scrape this back into the pan. Stir well and add extra water or stock if the soup seems too thick.

3 Bring the soup back to a boil. Stir in the pasta, lower the heat and simmer gently until *al dente*.

4 Heat the olive oil in a small pan. Add the garlic and sauté over low heat until golden. Stir into the soup with the parsley, and season well with salt and pepper. Ladle into warmed bowls and drizzle each with a little extra olive oil. Serve immediately.

> **Cook's Tip**
> *You can reduce the soaking time for the beans by putting them in a saucepan, covering with cold water and bringing very slowly to a boil over very low heat. Then boil for 2 minutes, remove from heat, cover and let soak for 1 hour.*

Tomato, Borlotti & Pasta Soup

This peasant soup is very thick. It should always be made with dried or fresh beans, never canned ones.

Serves 4–6

1½ cups dried borlotti or cannellini beans, soaked overnight in water to cover
14-ounce can chopped tomatoes
3 garlic cloves, crushed
2 bay leaves
pinch of coarsely ground black pepper
2 tablespoons olive oil
3 cups water
2 teaspoons tomato paste
2 teaspoons salt
1¾ cups dried ditalini or other small pasta shapes
3 tablespoons chopped fresh parsley
freshly grated Parmesan cheese, to serve (optional)

1 Drain the beans, rinse under cold water, then place them in a large saucepan. Pour in fresh water to cover. Bring to a boil and boil hard for 10 minutes. Drain, rinse and drain again.

2 Return the beans to the pan. Add enough water to cover them by 1 inch. Stir in the tomatoes, garlic, bay leaves, black pepper and oil. Bring to a boil, then simmer for 1½–2 hours or until the beans are tender. If necessary, add more water.

3 Remove and discard the bay leaves. Scoop out about half of the bean mixture and process into a purée in a food processor. Stir it back into the pan. Add the measured water and tomato paste, then bring the soup to a boil.

4 Add the salt and the pasta. Cook, stirring occasionally, until the pasta is *al dente*. Stir in the parsley. Let stand for at least 10 minutes before serving in warmed bowls. Serve with grated Parmesan passed separately, if using.

Crab & Egg Noodle Broth

This delicious broth takes only minutes to make and is both nutritious and filling.

Serves 4

3 ounces fine egg noodles
2 tablespoons butter
1 small bunch scallions, chopped
1 celery stalk, sliced
1 carrot, cut into batons
5 cups chicken stock
¼ cup dry sherry
4 ounces fresh or thawed frozen
    white crabmeat, flaked
pinch of celery salt
pinch of cayenne pepper
2 teaspoons lemon juice
1 small bunch cilantro or
    flat-leaf parsley, to garnish

1 Bring a large saucepan of salted water to a boil. Toss in the egg noodles and cook according to the instructions on the package. Drain, cool under cold running water and let sit immersed in water until needed.

2 Heat the butter in another large pan, add the scallions, celery and carrot, cover and cook the vegetables over low heat for 3–4 minutes, until softened.

3 Add the chicken stock and sherry, bring to a boil, then lower the heat and cook for 5 more minutes.

4 Drain the noodles and add to the broth, together with the crabmeat. Season to taste with celery salt and cayenne pepper, and sharpen with the lemon juice. Return to a simmer.

5 Ladle the broth into warmed shallow soup plates, sprinkle on roughly chopped cilantro or parsley and serve.

Cook's Tip
For the best flavor, buy a freshly cooked crab and remove the meat yourself. Frozen crabmeat, available at supermarkets, is a good substitute, but avoid canned crab, as it tastes rather bland and has a slightly soggy texture.

Variation
You could use other vegetables in season for this soup. Julienne strips of celeriac, broccoli spears or cauliflower florets would also work well.

Spicy Shrimp & Noodle Soup

Diners spoon noodles into their bowls, followed by the accompaniments, before ladling in the broth.

Serves 4–6

5 ounces rice vermicelli, soaked in
    warm water until soft
¼ cup cashews, chopped
3 shallots, sliced
2-inch piece of lemongrass,
    shredded
2 garlic cloves, crushed
1 tablespoon vegetable oil
1 tablespoon fish sauce
1 tablespoon mild curry paste
⅔ cup canned coconut milk
8 fluid ounces chicken stock
1 pound white fish fillet, cut into
    bite-size pieces
8 ounces shrimp, peeled
    and deveined
shrimp crackers, to serve

For the vegetable platter
1 small romaine lettuce, shredded
2 cups bean sprouts
3 scallions, shredded
½ cucumber, cut in
    matchstick strips

1 Drain the noodles. Cook them in a pan of lightly salted boiling water according to the package instructions. Cool under running water and let sit immersed in water until required.

2 Put the nuts in a mortar and grind them with a pestle. Add the shallots, lemongrass and garlic, and grind the mixture into a paste. Heat the oil in a large wok or pan and fry the paste for 1–2 minutes or until the nuts begin to brown.

3 Stir the fish sauce and curry paste into the fried paste, then add the coconut milk and chicken stock. Stir well, then bring to the simmering point. Simmer for 10 minutes.

4 Add the fish and shrimp. Cook for 3–4 minutes, until the shrimp have turned pink and the fish is translucent. Remove the seafood with a slotted spoon and arrange it in separate piles on a large platter. Drain the noodles well and heap them on the platter, with the vegetables and shrimp crackers in neat piles.

5 Pour the coconut stock into a tureen or earthenware pot and serve with the platter of seafood and vegetables.

Snapper & Tamarind Noodle Soup

Tamarind gives this light, fragrant noodle soup a slightly sour taste. It is available at Asian food stores and there is really no substitute.

Serves 4

8 cups water
1 whole red snapper or mullet, about 2¼ pounds, cleaned
1 onion, sliced
2 ounces tamarind pods
1 tablespoon fish sauce
1 tablespoon sugar
1 tablespoon vegetable oil
2 garlic cloves, finely chopped
2 lemongrass stalks, very finely chopped
4 ripe tomatoes, roughly chopped
2 tablespoons yellow bean paste
8 ounces rice vermicelli, soaked in warm water until soft
2 cups bean sprouts
8–10 fresh basil or mint sprigs
2 tablespoons roasted peanuts, finely chopped
salt and freshly ground black pepper

1 Bring the measured water to a boil in a large, heavy saucepan. Lower the heat and add the fish, with the onion slices and ½ teaspoon salt. Simmer over low heat until the fish is cooked through.

2 Carefully remove the fish from the stock and set it aside. Add the tamarind, fish sauce and sugar to the stock. Cook for about 5 minutes, then strain the stock into a large pitcher or bowl. Carefully remove all the bones from the fish, keeping the flesh in big pieces.

3 Heat the oil in a large frying pan. Add the garlic and lemongrass and stir-fry for a few seconds. Stir in the tomatoes and bean paste. Cook gently for 5–7 minutes, until the tomatoes have softened. Add the stock, bring back to a simmer and adjust the seasoning, if necessary.

4 Drain the vermicelli. Plunge it into a saucepan of boiling water for a few minutes, drain and divide among four warmed soup bowls. Add the bean sprouts, fish and basil or mint. Fill up each bowl with the hot soup and sprinkle the peanuts on top. Serve immediately.

Seafood Soup with Noodles

Described as a soup but very substantial, this would be an ideal choice for a late night, after-theater dinner with friends.

Serves 6

6 ounces tiger shrimp, peeled and deveined
8 ounces monkfish fillet, cut into chunks
8 ounces salmon fillet, cut into chunks
1 teaspoon vegetable oil
1 tablespoon dry white wine
8 ounces dried egg noodles
5 cups fish stock
1 carrot, thinly sliced
8 ounces asparagus, cut into 2-inch lengths
2 tablespoons dark soy sauce
1 teaspoon sesame oil
salt and freshly ground black pepper
2 scallions, cut into thin rings, to garnish

1 Mix the shrimp and fish in a bowl. Add the vegetable oil and wine with ¼ teaspoon salt and a little pepper. Mix lightly, cover and marinate in a cool place for 15 minutes.

2 Bring a large saucepan of water to a boil and cook the noodles for 4 minutes, until just tender, or according to the instructions on the package. Drain the noodles thoroughly and divide among six serving bowls. Keep hot.

3 Bring the fish stock to a boil in a separate pan. Add the shrimp and monkfish, cook for 1 minute, then add the salmon and cook for 2 more minutes.

4 Using a slotted spoon, carefully lift the fish and shrimp out of the fish stock, add to the noodles in the bowls and continue to keep hot.

5 Strain the stock through a sieve lined with muslin or cheesecloth into a clean pan. Bring to a boil and cook the carrot and asparagus for 2 minutes, then stir in the soy sauce and sesame oil.

6 Pour the stock and vegetables over the noodles and seafood, garnish with the scallions and serve immediately.

Noodle Soup with Pork & Pickle

A satisfying and warming soup from western China, a region famous for its delicious spicy pickles.

Serves 4

4 cups chicken stock
12 ounces dried medium
  egg noodles
1 tablespoon dried shrimp,
  soaked in water
1 tablespoon vegetable oil
8 ounces lean pork,
  finely shredded
1 tablespoon yellow bean paste
1 tablespoon soy sauce
4 ounces Szechuan hot pickle,
  rinsed, drained and shredded
pinch of sugar
salt and freshly ground
  black pepper
2 scallions, finely sliced,
  to garnish

1 Bring the chicken stock to a boil in a large saucepan. Add the egg noodles and cook until almost tender. Drain the dried shrimp, rinse under cold running water, drain again and add to the stock. Lower the heat and simmer for 2 minutes. Season to taste. Keep hot.

2 Heat the oil in a frying pan or wok. Add the pork and stir-fry over high heat for about 3 minutes.

3 Add the yellow bean paste and soy sauce to the pork and stir-fry for 1 minute, then add the hot pickle and sugar. Stir-fry for 1 more minute.

4 Divide the noodles and stock among warmed soup bowls. Spoon the pork mixture on top, then sprinkle with the scallions and serve immediately.

Cook's Tip
Available in cans at Chinese food stores, Szechuan hot pickle is based on kohlrabi. It has a very spicy and salty flavor. Other Chinese pickles that could be used include the milder winter pickle, made from salted cabbage and the sour snow pickle, made from salted mustard greens.

Hanoi Beef & Noodle Soup

Millions of Vietnamese people enjoy this fragrant and sustaining soup for breakfast.

Serves 4–6

1 onion
3–3 1/2 pounds beef shank
  with bones
1 bay leaf
1-inch piece of fresh ginger root
1 star anise
2 whole cloves
1/2 teaspoon fennel seeds
1 piece of cassia bark or
  cinnamon stick
12 cups water
dash of fish sauce
juice of 1 lime
5 ounces beef fillet
1 pound fresh flat rice noodles
salt

**For the garnish
accompaniments**
1 small red onion, sliced into rings
2 cups bean sprouts
2 fresh red chiles, seeded
  and sliced
2 scallions, finely sliced
a handful of cilantro leaves
lime wedges

1 Cut the onion in half. Broil under high heat, cut-side up, until the exposed sides are caramelized and deep brown. Set aside.

2 Cut the meat into large chunks and place with the bones in a large saucepan. Add the caramelized onion, bay leaf, ginger, star anise, cloves, fennel seeds and cassia bark or cinnamon.

3 Pour in the measured water, bring to a boil, then lower the heat and simmer for 2–3 hours, skimming occasionally.

4 Remove the meat from the stock. When cool enough to handle, cut it into small pieces, discarding the bones. Strain the stock and return to the pan with the meat. Bring back to a boil and season with the fish sauce and lime juice.

5 Slice the beef fillet very thinly. Place the garnishes in separate serving bowls. Cook the noodles in a large saucepan of lightly salted boiling water until *al dente*. Drain and divide among warmed bowls. Top with the beef, ladle on hot stock and serve, passing the accompaniments separately.

Pasta, Melon & Shrimp Salad

Orange-fleshed cantaloupe
or Charentais melon looks
spectacular in this salad.

Serves 4–6
1½ cups dried pasta shapes
1 large melon
8 ounces cooked peeled shrimp

2 tablespoons olive oil
1 tablespoon tarragon vinegar
2 tablespoons snipped fresh
    chives or chopped parsley
shredded Chinese cabbage
fresh herb sprigs, to garnish

1 Bring a large pan of lightly salted water to a boil and cook the pasta until it is *al dente*. Drain, rinse under cold water and drain again. Put it into a bowl and leave until cold.

2 Cut the melon in half and remove the seeds with a teaspoon. Carefully scoop the flesh into balls with a melon baller and add to the pasta, with the shrimp.

3 Whisk the oil, vinegar and chopped herbs in a bowl. Pour onto the shrimp mixture and turn to coat. Cover and chill for at least 30 minutes.

4 Line a shallow serving bowl with the shredded Chinese cabbage, pile the shrimp mixture on top and garnish with the herb sprigs. Serve immediately.

> **Cook's Tip**
> *For an attractive presentation, serve the salad in the melon shells, lined with the Chinese cabbage.*

> **Variation**
> • *For a really special treat, substitute chopped cooked lobster meat for the shrimp.*
> • *For a different flavor and texture, use a mixture of Ogen, cantaloupe and watermelon.*

Crab Pasta Salad with Spicy Cocktail Dressing

A variation on a very
popular appetizer, this salad
is certain to go over well.

salt and freshly ground
    black pepper
fresh basil, to garnish

Serves 6
3 cups dried fusilli
1 small red bell pepper, seeded
    and finely chopped
2 6-ounce cans white
    crabmeat, drained
4 ounces cherry tomatoes, halved
¼ cucumber, halved, seeded and
    sliced into crescents
1 tablespoon lemon juice

For the dressing
1¼ cups low-fat plain yogurt
2 celery stalks, finely chopped
2 teaspoons horseradish cream
½ teaspoon ground paprika
½ teaspoon Dijon mustard
2 tablespoons sweet tomato
    pickle or chutney

1 Bring a large pan of lightly salted water to a boil and cook the pasta until it is *al dente*. Drain, rinse under cold water, and drain again.

2 Put the chopped red pepper in a heatproof bowl and pour over boiling water to cover. Let stand for 1 minute, then drain, rinse under cold water and drain again. Pat dry on paper towels.

3 Drain the crabmeat and pick over it carefully, removing any stray pieces of shell. Put the crabmeat into a bowl, and add the tomatoes and cucumber. Season with salt and pepper to taste, then sprinkle with the lemon juice.

4 Make the dressing. Put the yogurt, celery, horseradish cream, paprika, mustard and pickle or chutney into a bowl and mix well. Season with salt, if necessary.

5 Stir in the diced red pepper and the pasta. Transfer the mixture to a serving dish. Spoon the crab mixture on top and mix well. Garnish with fresh basil and serve.

Curried Chicken Salad with Penne

There are several versions of this popular salad. This one has a dressing based on low-fat yogurt, so it is a relatively healthy option.

Serves 4
2 cooked boneless, skinless
   chicken breasts
6 ounces green beans, trimmed
   and cut in short lengths
3 cups dried penne, preferably
   mixed colors
⅔ cup low-fat yogurt
1 teaspoon mild curry powder
1 garlic clove, crushed
1 fresh green chile, seeded and
   finely chopped
2 tablespoons chopped cilantro
4 firm ripe tomatoes, peeled,
   seeded and cut in strips
salt and freshly ground
   black pepper
cilantro leaves, to garnish

1 Cut the chicken breasts into bite-size pieces. Bring a large pan of lightly salted water to a boil and cook the green beans for 2–3 minutes. Lift them into a colander, using a slotted spoon, and drain under cold water. Drain again.

2 Bring the water back to a boil and cook the pasta until it is *al dente*. Drain, rinse under cold water and drain again.

3 Mix the yogurt, curry powder, garlic, chile and chopped cilantro together in a bowl. Stir in the chicken pieces and let stand for 30 minutes.

4 Put the pasta in a glass bowl, and toss with the beans and tomatoes. Spoon on the chicken and sauce. Garnish with cilantro leaves and serve.

> **Variation**
> For an alternative dressing, combine ⅔ cup mayonnaise, 2 teaspoons concentrated curry sauce, ½ teaspoon lemon juice and 2 teaspoons sieved apricot jam. Add the chicken to the dressing and chill in the refrigerator for 30 minutes before mixing with the pasta and serving.

Marinated Chicken & Pasta Salad

This tastes good when the chicken is served warm, but it can be served cold, if that is more convenient.

Serves 6
1 teaspoon ground cumin seeds
1 teaspoon ground paprika
1 teaspoon ground turmeric
1–2 garlic cloves, crushed
3–4 tablespoons fresh
   lime juice
4 skinless, boneless
   chicken breasts
2 cups dried rigatoni
1 red bell pepper, seeded
   and chopped
2 celery stalks, thinly sliced
1 small onion, finely chopped
6 stuffed green olives, halved
2 tablespoons honey
1 tablespoon whole-grain mustard
salt and freshly ground
   black pepper
mixed salad leaves, to serve

1 Mix the cumin, paprika, turmeric, garlic and 2 tablespoons of the lime juice in a bowl. Season to taste with a little salt and pepper. Rub this mixture onto the chicken breasts. Lay them in a shallow dish, cover with plastic wrap and set in a cool place for about 3 hours or overnight.

2 Preheat the oven to 400°F. Place the chicken breasts in a single layer on a rack set over a roasting pan. Bake for 20 minutes.

3 Meanwhile, bring a large pan of lightly salted water to a boil and cook the rigatoni until *al dente*. Drain, rinse under cold water and drain again. Leave until cold.

4 Put the red pepper, celery, onion and olives into a large bowl. Add the pasta and mix carefully.

5 Mix the honey, mustard and the remaining lime juice to taste in a bowl. Pour the mixture over the pasta. Toss to coat.

6 Cut the chicken into bite-size pieces. Arrange the mixed salad leaves on a serving dish, spoon the pasta mixture into the center, top with the spicy chicken pieces and serve.

Duck & Rigatoni Salad

This sophisticated salad has a delicious sweet-sour dressing that goes wonderfully well with the richness of duck.

Serves 6

2 duck breasts, boned
1 teaspoon coriander
  seeds, crushed
3 cups rigatoni
⅔ cup fresh orange juice
1 tablespoon lemon juice
2 teaspoons honey
1 shallot, finely chopped
1 garlic clove, crushed
1 celery stalk, chopped
3 ounces dried cherries
3 tablespoons port
1 tablespoon chopped fresh mint,
  plus extra to garnish
2 tablespoons chopped cilantro,
  plus extra to garnish
1 apple, diced
2 oranges, segmented
salt and freshly ground
  black pepper

1 Preheat the broiler. Remove the skin and fat from the duck breasts, and season them with salt and pepper. Rub them with the crushed coriander seeds. Place them on a broiler rack and broil for 7–10 minutes. Wrap them in foil and set aside for 20 minutes.

2 Bring a large pan of lightly salted water to a boil and cook the pasta until it is *al dente*. Drain, rinse under cold water and drain again. Let cool.

3 Put the orange juice, lemon juice, honey, shallot, garlic, celery, cherries, port, mint and cilantro into a bowl, whisk together and let the dressing stand for 30 minutes.

4 Slice the duck very thinly. (It should be pink in the center.) Put the pasta into a bowl, add the dressing, apple and oranges. Toss well. Transfer the salad to a serving plate. Add the duck slices, and garnish with the extra cilantro and mint.

Cook's Tip
If you do not like your duck pink in the middle, then broil it for a little longer.

Deviled Ham & Pineapple Penne Salad

Ham and pineapple are often paired. In this salad, the combination works particularly well, thanks to the fruity dressing.

Serves 4

2 cups whole-wheat penne
⅔ cup low-fat plain yogurt
1 tablespoon cider vinegar
1 teaspoon whole-grain mustard
a large pinch of sugar
2 tablespoons hot mango chutney
4 ounces cooked ham, diced
7-ounce can natural pineapple
  chunks, drained
2 celery stalks, chopped
½ green bell pepper, seeded
  and diced
1 tablespoon sliced toasted
  almonds, roughly chopped
salt and freshly ground
  black pepper

1 Bring a large pan of lightly salted water to a boil and cook the pasta until it is *al dente*. Drain, rinse under cold water and drain again. Let cool.

2 Mix the yogurt, vinegar, mustard, sugar and mango chutney in a large bowl. Add the pasta, and season with salt and pepper to taste. Toss lightly together.

3 Pile the dressed pasta onto a serving dish. Sprinkle on the ham, pineapple, celery and green pepper.

4 Sprinkle the toasted almonds on top. Serve immediately.

Variations
• *Substitute garlic croutons for the toasted almonds to garnish the salad.*
• *Instead of pineapple chunks, you could use chopped fresh or canned mangoes.*
• *Add a diced green apple with the celery and green bell pepper in step 3.*

Bacon & Bean Pasta Salad

This tasty pasta salad is subtly flavored with smoked bacon in a light, flavorful dressing.

Serves 4
8 ounces green beans
3 cups dried whole-wheat fusilli
  or spirali
8 strips bacon
12 ounces cherry
  tomatoes, halved
2 bunches of scallions, chopped

14-ounce can chickpeas, rinsed
  and drained
6 tablespoons tomato juice
2 tablespoons balsamic vinegar
1 teaspoon ground cumin
1 teaspoon ground coriander
2 tablespoons chopped cilantro
salt and freshly ground
  black pepper

1 Bring a large pan of lightly salted water to a boil and cook the beans for 3–4 minutes, until crisp-tender. Lift them out with a slotted spoon and place in a colander. Refresh under cold water and drain.

2 Bring the water back to a boil, add the pasta and cook until *al dente*.

3 Meanwhile, broil the bacon until crisp. Dice or crumble it and add it to the beans.

4 Mix the tomatoes, scallions and chickpeas in a large bowl. In a bowl, combine the tomato juice, vinegar, cumin, ground coriander and cilantro, and season to taste with salt and pepper. Pour the dressing onto the tomato mixture.

5 Drain the pasta thoroughly and add it to the tomato mixture with the beans and bacon. Toss well. Serve warm or cold.

Variation
You could substitute canned navy beans or flageolets for the chickpeas.

Herbed Beef & Pasta Salad

Fillet of beef is such a luxury cut that it makes sense to stretch it if you can. Serving it as part of a pasta salad is an excellent way of doing this.

Serves 6
1 pound beef fillet
1 pound fresh tagliatelle
  with herbs
½ cucumber
4 ounces cherry tomatoes, halved

For the marinade
1 tablespoon soy sauce
1 tablespoon sherry
1 teaspoon fresh ginger
  root, grated
1 garlic clove, crushed

For the herb dressing
2–3 tablespoons
  horseradish sauce
⅔ cup low-fat plain yogurt
1 garlic clove, crushed
2–3 tablespoons chopped
  fresh herbs
salt and freshly ground
  black pepper

1 Mix all the marinade ingredients in a shallow dish, add the beef and turn it over to coat it. Cover with plastic wrap and leave for 30 minutes to let the flavors penetrate the meat.

2 Preheat the broiler. Lift the fillet out of the marinade and pat it dry with paper towels. Place it on a broiler rack and broil for 8 minutes on each side, basting with the marinade during cooking, then put it on a plate, cover with aluminum foil and let stand for 20 minutes.

3 Bring a pan of lightly salted water to a boil, add the pasta and cook until it is *al dente*. Drain, rinse under cold water and drain again.

4 Cut the cucumber in half lengthwise, scoop out the seeds with a teaspoon and slice the flesh thinly into crescents.

5 Mix all the dressing ingredients in a large bowl. Add the pasta, cucumber and cherry tomatoes, and toss to coat. Divide among six plates. Slice the beef thinly and fan out the slices alongside the salad. Serve immediately.

Potato & Cellophane Noodle Salad

Asian noodles aren't the obvious choice for salads in the West, but perhaps they should be, as they add a new dimension.

Serves 4

2 medium potatoes, peeled and
    cut into eighths
6 ounces cellophane noodles,
    soaked in hot water until soft
2 tablespoons vegetable oil
1 onion, finely sliced
1 teaspoon ground turmeric
1/4 cup graham flour
1 teaspoon grated lemon zest
4–5 tablespoons lemon juice
3 tablespoons Thai fish sauce
4 scallions, finely sliced
salt and freshly ground black
    pepper (optional)

1 Place the potatoes in a saucepan. Add lightly salted water to cover, bring to a boil and cook for about 15 minutes, until tender but not soggy. Drain and set aside to cool.

2 Meanwhile, bring a second pan of lightly salted water to a boil. Drain the soaked noodles, add them to the water and cook briefly, until they are just tender. Drain, rinse under cold running water and drain again.

3 Heat the oil in a frying pan and sauté the onion with the turmeric for about 5 minutes, until golden brown. Drain the onion, reserving the oil.

4 Heat a small frying pan. Add the graham flour and stir constantly for about 4 minutes, until it turns light golden brown.

5 Mix the drained potatoes, noodles and cooked onion in a large bowl. Add the reserved oil and the toasted graham flour with the lemon zest and juice, fish sauce and scallions. Combine well and adjust the seasoning if necessary. Serve immediately.

> **Cook's Tip**
> *Cellophane noodles need very little cooking and will probably be ready in 1–2 minutes. Check the instructions on the package.*

Buckwheat Noodles with Smoked Salmon

The slightly earthy flavor of buckwheat noodles complements the smoked salmon perfectly in this warm salad.

Serves 4

8 ounces buckwheat or
    soba noodles
1 tablespoon oyster sauce
juice of 1/2 lemon
2 tablespoons light olive oil
4 ounces smoked salmon, cut into
    thin strips
2 cups young pea sprouts
2 ripe tomatoes, peeled, seeded
    and cut into strips
1 tablespoon snipped chives
salt and freshly ground
    black pepper

1 Bring a large pan of lightly salted water to a boil and cook the noodles until just tender, checking the package for instructions on timing. Drain, rinse under cold water and drain again.

2 Put the noodles in a large bowl. Add the oyster sauce and lemon juice, and season with pepper to taste. Moisten with the olive oil.

3 Add the smoked salmon, pea sprouts, tomatoes and chives. Mix well and serve immediately.

> **Variations**
> *• Young pea sprouts are only available for a short time. You can substitute watercress, young leeks or your favorite green vegetable or herb.*
> *• This recipe would also be delicious made with buckling or smoked eel instead of salmon.*

Sesame Duck & Noodle Salad

The marinade for this main-course salad contains a delicious blend of spices.

Serves 4
2 duck breasts, thinly sliced
1 tablespoon oil
8 ounces medium dried
  egg noodles
5 ounces sugar snap peas
2 carrots, cut into 3-inch sticks
6 scallions, sliced
salt
2 tablespoons cilantro leaves,
  to garnish

For the marinade
1 tablespoon sesame oil
1 teaspoon ground cilantro
1 teaspoon Chinese
  five-spice powder

For the dressing
1 tablespoon garlic vinegar or
  balsamic vinegar
1 teaspoon light brown sugar
1 teaspoon soy sauce
1 tablespoon toasted
  sesame seeds
2 tablespoons sunflower oil
1 tablespoon sesame oil
ground black pepper

1 Place the duck in a shallow dish. Mix all the ingredients for the marinade. Pour the mixture onto the duck and use your hands to rub in the mixture. Cover and set aside for 30 minutes.

2 Heat the oil in a frying pan, add the slices of duck breast and stir-fry them for 3–4 minutes, until cooked. Set aside.

3 Bring a saucepan of lightly salted water to a boil. Add the noodles, place the sugar snap peas and carrots in a steamer on top and cook for the time suggested on the noodle package. Set the vegetables aside. Drain the noodles, refresh them under cold running water and drain again. Put them in a large serving bowl.

4 Make the dressing. Mix the vinegar, sugar, soy sauce and toasted sesame seeds. Season with ground black pepper and whisk in the oils.

5 Pour the dressing onto the noodles and mix well. Add the sugar snap peas, carrots, scallions and duck slices, and toss to mix. Sprinkle on the cilantro leaves and serve.

Curry Fried Pork & Noodle Salad

This popular salad combines an interesting variety of flavors and textures.

Serves 4
8 ounces pork fillet, trimmed
2 garlic cloves, finely chopped
2 slices of fresh ginger root,
  finely chopped
2–3 tablespoons rice wine
1 tablespoon vegetable oil
2 lemongrass stalks,
  finely chopped
2 teaspoons curry powder
3 cups bean sprouts

8 ounces rice vermicelli, soaked in
  warm water until soft
1/2 lettuce, finely shredded
2 tablespoons fresh mint leaves
lemon juice
Thai fish sauce
salt and freshly ground
  black pepper

To garnish
2 scallions, chopped
1/4 cup roasted peanuts, chopped
pork crackling (optional)

1 Cut the pork into thin strips. Place these in a shallow dish with half the garlic and ginger. Season with salt and pepper, pour on 2 tablespoons of the rice wine, stir and marinate for 1 hour.

2 Heat the oil in a frying pan. Add the remaining garlic and ginger, and sauté for a few seconds until fragrant. Stir in the pork, with the marinade, and add the lemongrass and curry powder. Cook until the pork is golden and cooked through, adding more rice wine if the mixture seems too dry.

3 Meanwhile, blanch the bean sprouts in boiling water for 1 minute. Drain, refresh under cold water and drain again.

4 Using the same water, cook the drained rice vermicelli for 3–5 minutes, until tender. Drain and rinse under cold running water. Drain well and put in a bowl.

5 Add the bean sprouts, shredded lettuce and mint to the bowl. Season with lemon juice and fish sauce to taste. Toss lightly. Divide the noodle mixture among individual plates. Arrange the pork mixture on top. Garnish with scallions, roasted peanuts and pork crackling, if using.

FISH & SHELLFISH

Tuna & Mixed Vegetable Pasta

Mushrooms, tuna and pasta make a tasty combination, and the fat content is satisfyingly low.

Serves 4
1 tablespoon olive oil
2 cups sliced button mushrooms
1 garlic clove, crushed
1/2 red bell pepper, seeded and chopped
1 tablespoon tomato paste
1 1/4 cups tomato juice

1 cup frozen peas
1–2 tablespoons drained pickled green peppercorns, crushed
2 1/2 cups whole-wheat pasta shapes
7-ounce can tuna chunks in water, drained
6 scallions, diagonally sliced
salt

1 Heat the olive oil in a heavy saucepan. Add the mushrooms, garlic and red pepper, and sauté gently over low heat until softened.

2 Stir in the tomato paste, then add the tomato juice, peas and some or all of the crushed peppercorns, depending on how spicy you want the sauce. Bring to a boil, lower the heat and simmer.

3 Bring a large pan of lightly salted water to a boil and cook the pasta until *al dente*.

4 When the pasta is almost ready, add the tuna to the sauce and heat through gently. Stir in the scallions. Drain the pasta, put it in a heated bowl and pour on the sauce. Serve immediately.

Variations
• *Substitute 2/3 cup frozen or canned corn kernels for the peas.*
• *Use canned or flaked smoked mackerel fillets instead of the canned tuna.*

Conchiglie with Tomato & Tuna Sauce

The trick with low-fat food is to make it as flavorful as you can, using aromatics, herbs and extra flavorings such as capers.

Serves 6
1 medium onion, finely chopped
1 celery stalk, finely chopped
1 red bell pepper, seeded and diced
1 garlic clove, crushed
2/3 cup vegetable stock
14-ounce can chopped tomatoes
1 tablespoon tomato paste

2 teaspoons sugar
1 tablespoon chopped fresh basil
1 tablespoon chopped fresh parsley
4 cups dried conchiglie
14-ounce can tuna in water, drained
2 tablespoons bottled capers in vinegar, drained
salt and freshly ground black pepper

1 Put the onion, celery, red pepper and garlic into a large nonstick pan. Add the vegetable stock, bring to a boil and cook over medium heat for about 5 minutes or until most of the stock has evaporated and very little liquid remains.

2 Stir in the tomatoes, tomato paste, sugar, basil and parsley. Season to taste with salt and pepper, and bring to a boil over medium heat.

3 Lower the heat and simmer the sauce for 30 minutes, until thickened, stirring occasionally.

4 Meanwhile, bring a large pan of lightly salted water to a boil and cook the pasta until *al dente*. Drain thoroughly and transfer to a warm serving dish.

5 Flake the tuna into large chunks and add it to the sauce with the capers. Heat gently, stirring occasionally but without breaking up the fish, for 1–2 minutes. Pour over the pasta, toss gently and serve immediately.

Pasta with Tuna, Capers & Anchovies

This piquant sauce could be made without tomatoes—just heat the oil, add the other ingredients and heat through gently before tossing with the pasta.

Serves 4

1 tablespoon olive oil
2 garlic cloves, crushed
2 14-ounce cans
 chopped tomatoes
14-ounce can tuna in
 water, drained
6 drained canned anchovy fillets
2 tablespoons drained bottled
 capers in vinegar
2 tablespoons chopped fresh basil
4 cups dried rigatoni, penne
 or garganelli
salt and freshly ground
 black pepper
fresh basil sprigs, to garnish

1 Heat the olive oil in a heavy saucepan. Add the garlic and cook over medium heat until golden, but not browned. Lower the heat, stir in the tomatoes and simmer for about 25 minutes, until thickened.

2 Flake the tuna and cut the anchovies in half. Stir the fish into the sauce with the capers and chopped basil. Season well with salt and pepper.

3 Bring a large pan of lightly salted water to a boil and cook the pasta until it is *al dente*.

4 Drain the pasta well, return to the clean pan and toss with the sauce. Serve immediately in warmed bowls, garnished with the fresh basil sprigs.

Cook's Tip
Olive oil is high in monounsaturated fats and so is a healthy choice. However, if you want to cut the fat content of this dish still further, omit it and coat the bottom of the pan very thinly with light spray oil.

Salmon Pasta with Parsley Sauce

Delicately flavored and with a lovely color, salmon makes a surprisingly substantial meal, especially when tossed with pasta shapes.

Serves 4

1 pound salmon fillet, skinned
2/3 cup very low-fat fromage frais
3 tablespoons finely
 chopped parsley
finely grated zest of 1/2 orange
2 cups dried penne or spirali
6 ounces cherry tomatoes, halved
salt and freshly ground
 black pepper

1 Cut the salmon into bite-size pieces, arrange on a heatproof plate and cover with aluminum foil. Mix the fromage frais, parsley and orange zest in a bowl, and stir in pepper to taste.

2 Bring a large pan of lightly salted water to a boil, add the pasta and return to a boil. Lower the heat, place the plate of salmon on top and simmer for 10–12 minutes or until both the pasta and salmon are cooked.

3 Lift off the plate of salmon and drain the pasta well. Put the pasta in a bowl and toss with the fromage frais mixture until coated. Add the tomatoes and salmon, and toss again, taking care not to break up the fish too much. Serve hot or cold.

Cook's Tip
Salmon is an oily fish and contains 8–12 percent fat, mostly in the form of Omega 3 fatty acids, which are believed to be beneficial in helping to prevent coronary heart disease. In this recipe, the fat content of the fish is counterbalanced by using very low-fat or even virtually fat-free fromage frais.

Spaghetti with Hot-and-Sour Fish

Hoisin sauce is the secret ingredient that makes this taste so good.

Serves 4

1 tablespoon olive oil
1 large onion, chopped
1 teaspoon ground turmeric
1 fresh green chile, cored, seeded and finely chopped
8 ounces zucchini, thinly sliced
1 cup shelled peas, thawed if frozen
12 ounces dried spaghetti
1 pound monkfish tail, skinned and cut into bite-size pieces
2 teaspoons lemon juice
5 tablespoons hoi-sin sauce
⅔ cup water
salt and freshly ground black pepper
a sprig of fresh dill, to garnish

1 Heat the oil in a large frying pan and sauté the onion for 5 minutes, until softened. Stir in the turmeric and cook for 1 more minute.

2 Add the chile, zucchini and peas, and cook over low heat until the vegetables have softened.

3 Meanwhile, bring a large saucepan of lightly salted water to a boil, add the spaghetti and cook until it is *al dente*.

4 Stir the fish, lemon juice, hoisin sauce and water into the vegetable mixture. Bring to a boil, then lower the heat and simmer for 5 minutes or until the fish is tender. Season to taste with salt and pepper.

5 Drain the spaghetti thoroughly and put it in a serving bowl. Add the sauce and toss to coat. Serve immediately, garnished with a sprig of fresh dill.

> **Cook's Tip**
> *Monkfish tail is quite often skinned before it is displayed for sale. Nevertheless, it is still essential to strip off the transparent membrane surrounding the flesh, as this will become tough on cooking.*

Tagliatelle with Cucumber & Smoked Salmon

The light texture of the cucumber complements the fish perfectly in this summery dish.

Serves 4

½ cucumber
12 ounces dried tagliatelle
2 tablespoons butter
grated zest of 1 orange
2 tablespoons chopped fresh dill
1¼ cups low-fat crème fraîche
1 tablespoon freshly squeezed orange juice
4 ounces smoked salmon, skinned and cut into thin strips
salt and freshly ground black pepper

1 Cut the cucumber in half lengthwise, then, using a small spoon, scoop out and discard the seeds from the center. Slice the cucumber thinly.

2 Bring a large pan of lightly salted water to a boil, add the tagliatelle and cook until *al dente*.

3 Melt the butter in a heavy saucepan and stir in the orange zest and dill. Add the cucumber and cook over low heat, stirring occasionally, for about 2 minutes.

4 Pour in the low-fat crème fraîche and orange juice, season with salt and pepper to taste and simmer for 1 minute, then stir in the salmon and heat through.

5 Drain the pasta, return it to the pan and add the sauce. Toss lightly to coat. Serve immediately.

> **Cook's Tip**
> *An economical way to make this sauce is to use smoked salmon scraps, available at most supermarkets and delicatessens, as they are much cheaper than slices. Smoked trout is also a less expensive alternative.*

Fusilli with Smoked Trout

Curly strands of fusilli in a sauce that tastes deceptively creamy are topped with crisp-tender vegetables and smoked fish to make a dish that tastes every bit as good as it looks.

Serves 4–6

2 carrots, cut into
   matchstick strips
1 leek, cut into matchstick strips
2 celery stalks, cut into
   matchstick strips

²⁄₃ cup vegetable stock
8 ounces smoked trout fillets,
   skinned and cut into strips
scant 1 cup low-fat cream cheese
²⁄₃ cup medium sweet white wine
   or fish stock
1 tablespoon chopped fresh dill
   or fennel
8 ounces dried fusilli lunghi
salt and freshly ground
   black pepper
fresh dill sprigs, to garnish

1 Put the carrots, leek and celery into a pan. Pour in the vegetable stock. Bring to a boil and cook over high heat for 4–5 minutes, until the vegetables are tender and most of the stock has evaporated. Remove the pan from heat and add the smoked trout.

2 To make the sauce, put the cream cheese and white wine or fish stock into a large pan, and whisk over low heat until smooth. Season to taste with salt and pepper. Add the chopped dill or fennel.

3 Bring a large pan of lightly salted water to a boil and cook the pasta until *al dente*.

4 Drain the pasta well and add it to the pan with the sauce. Toss lightly, then transfer to a warmed serving bowl. Top with the cooked vegetables and trout. Serve immediately, garnished with dill sprigs.

Variation
Use smoked monkfish instead of trout.

Smoked Trout Cannelloni

Simmering vegetables in stock instead of frying them in fat or oil produces tasty, moist results.

Serves 4–6

1 large onion, finely chopped
1 garlic clove, crushed
¼ cup vegetable stock
2 14-ounce cans
   chopped tomatoes
½ teaspoon mixed dried herbs
1 smoked trout,
   about 14 ounces
¾ cup frozen peas, thawed

1½ cups fresh white
   bread crumbs
16 cannelloni tubes
salt and freshly ground
   black pepper

For the cheese sauce
2 tablespoons low-fat spread
¼ cup all-purpose flour
1½ cups skim milk
freshly grated nutmeg
3 tablespoons freshly grated
   Parmesan cheese

1 Put the onion, garlic and stock in a large pan. Cover and cook for 3 minutes. Remove the lid and continue to cook, stirring occasionally, until the stock has reduced entirely. Stir in the tomatoes and dried herbs. Simmer, uncovered, for 10 more minutes or until very thick.

2 Meanwhile, skin the fish, flake the flesh and discard the bones. Put the fish in a bowl and stir in the tomato mixture, peas and bread crumbs, and season to taste. Let cool slightly.

3 Preheat the oven to 375°F. Spoon the filling into the cannelloni tubes and arrange them in a single layer in an ovenproof dish.

4 Make the sauce. Put the low-fat spread, flour and milk into a pan and cook over medium heat, whisking constantly, until the sauce thickens. Simmer for 2–3 minutes, stirring constantly. Season to taste with salt, pepper and nutmeg.

5 Pour the sauce onto the cannelloni and sprinkle with the Parmesan. Bake for 35–40 minutes or until the top is golden and bubbling. Let stand for 5–10 minutes before serving.

Penne with Salmon & Dill

Rosé wine accentuates the color of the salmon and gives this simple dish a hint of sophistication.

Serves 6
12 ounces fresh salmon
   fillet, skinned
4 ounces sliced smoked salmon
3 cups dried penne
1–2 shallots, finely chopped

1 1/2 cups button
   mushrooms, quartered
2/3 cup rosé wine
2/3 cup fish stock
2/3 cup low-fat crème fraîche
2 tablespoons chopped fresh dill
salt and freshly ground
   black pepper
fresh dill sprigs, to garnish

1 Cut the fresh salmon into 1-inch cubes. Cut the smoked salmon into 1/2-inch strips and set aside.

2 Bring a large pan of lightly salted water to a boil and cook the pasta until it is *al dente*.

3 Meanwhile, put the shallots and mushrooms into a nonstick pan and pour in the rosé wine. Bring to a boil over medium heat and cook for about 5 minutes or until the wine has reduced almost completely.

4 Pour in the fish stock and crème fraîche, and stir until smooth. Add the fresh salmon, cover the pan and simmer gently over low heat for 2–3 minutes or until the salmon is cooked.

5 Drain the pasta and put it in a warmed serving dish. Add the smoked salmon and dill to the sauce, season to taste with salt and pepper, and pour onto the pasta. Toss lightly to mix. Serve immediately, garnished with the dill sprigs.

Variation
Use fresh and smoked trout instead of the salmon. Substitute red wine for the rosé, as trout does not have the same delicate pink coloring as salmon.

Tagliatelle with Smoked Trout & Dill

This light pasta dish can also be made with canned tuna or salmon for a convenient midweek dinner.

Serves 4
12 ounces fresh or
   dried tagliatelle
10 ounces smoked trout fillet,
   skinned and flaked
8 ounces cherry tomatoes, halved
2/3 cup low-fat fromage frais or
   low-fat plain yogurt
2 tablespoons chopped fresh dill
2 tablespoons chopped fresh chives
salt and freshly ground
   black pepper

1 Bring a large pan of lightly salted water to a boil and cook the pasta until *al dente*. Drain well and return to the clean pan.

2 Toss the flaked trout into the hot pasta, and add the tomatoes and fromage frais or yogurt.

3 Heat gently, without boiling, then stir in the herbs and season with black pepper to taste. Spoon into warmed bowls and serve immediately.

Cook's Tip
Low-fat fromage frais can frequently be used instead of cream in sauces, so consider this low-fat option in other recipes too.

Variation
Substitute pappardelle for the tagliatelle and smoked mackerel for the smoked trout. Omit the cherry tomatoes and add strips of red bell pepper instead. Toss the dressed pasta with finely diced cucumber rather than dill.

Spaghetti with Salmon & Shrimp

Light and fresh-tasting, this is perfect for an *al fresco* meal in summer. Serve with warm ciabatta.

Serves 4
11 ounces salmon fillet
scant 1 cup dry
    white wine
a few fresh basil sprigs, plus extra
    basil leaves, to garnish
6 ripe Italian plum tomatoes,
    peeled and finely chopped
2/3 cup very low-fat fromage frais
12 ounces fresh or
    dried spaghetti
4 ounces cooked peeled shrimp,
    thawed if frozen
salt and freshly ground
    black pepper

1 Put the salmon skin-side up in a wide shallow pan. Pour in the wine, then add the basil sprigs. Sprinkle the fish with salt and pepper. Bring to a boil, cover and simmer gently for no more than 5 minutes. Using a spatula, lift the fish out of the pan and set it aside to cool a little.

2 Stir the tomatoes and fromage frais into the liquid remaining in the pan and heat gently, without letting the sauce approach the boiling point. Meanwhile, bring a large pan of lightly salted water to a boil. Add the pasta and cook until *al dente*.

3 Flake the fish into large chunks, discarding the skin and any bones. Add the fish to the sauce with the shrimp, shaking the pan until they are well coated. Taste for seasoning.

4 Drain the pasta and put it in a warmed bowl. Pour the sauce on the pasta and toss to combine. Serve immediately, garnished with the fresh basil leaves.

Cook's Tip
Check the salmon fillet carefully for small bones when you are flaking the flesh. Although the salmon is already filleted, you will always find a few stray "pin" bones. Pick them out carefully, using tweezers or your fingertips.

Linguine with Smoked Salmon & Mushrooms

Proof positive that pasta dishes need not be high in fat, even when their sauces seem very creamy.

Serves 6
2 tablespoons olive oil
1 1/4 cups button mushrooms,
    thinly sliced
1 cup dry white wine
1 1/2 teaspoons fresh dill or
    1 teaspoon dried dill weed
handful of fresh chives, snipped
1 1/4 cups low-fat fromage frais
8 ounces smoked salmon, cut into
    thin strips
lemon juice
12 ounces fresh linguine
    or spaghetti
salt and freshly ground
    black pepper
whole fresh chives, to garnish

1 Heat the oil in a wide, shallow saucepan. Add the mushrooms and sauté over low heat for 4–5 minutes, until they have softened but not colored.

2 Pour the white wine into the pan. Increase the heat and boil rapidly for about 5 minutes, until the wine has reduced.

3 Stir in the herbs and fromage frais. Fold in the salmon and reheat gently. Stir in pepper and lemon juice to taste. Cover the pan and keep the sauce warm.

4 Bring a large saucepan of lightly salted water to a boil, add the pasta and cook until it is *al dente*. Drain, rinse thoroughly in boiling water and drain again. Turn into a warmed serving dish. Toss gently with the salmon sauce. Serve in warmed bowls, garnished with chives.

Cook's Tip
After you have added the fromage frais to the sauce, do not let it boil or it will curdle.

Smoked Haddock in Parsley Sauce

Perfect for a family dinner, this would be lovely with roasted tomatoes.

Serves 4

1 pound smoked haddock fillet
1 small leek or onion, thickly sliced
1¼ cups skim milk
1 bouquet garni (bay leaf, thyme and parsley stems)
2 cups dried conchiglie
2 tablespoons low-fat spread
¼ cup all-purpose flour
2 tablespoons chopped fresh parsley
salt and freshly ground black pepper
toasted sliced almonds, to serve (optional)

1 Remove the skin and any bones from the haddock. Put it into a pan with the leek or onion, milk and bouquet garni. Bring to the simmering point, cover and cook gently for 8–10 minutes, until the fish flakes easily when tested with the tip of a sharp knife.

2 Strain, reserving the cooking liquid, and discard the bouquet garni. Flake the fish and set it aside with the leek or onion.

3 Bring a large pan of lightly salted water to a boil and cook the pasta until it is *al dente*.

4 Meanwhile, put the low-fat spread and flour in a pan. Whisk in the milk used for cooking the fish. Bring to a boil over low heat, whisking until smooth. Season with salt and pepper to taste, and add the flaked fish and leek or onion.

5 Drain the pasta thoroughly and put it in a warmed serving bowl. Add the sauce and chopped parsley. Toss well. Serve immediately. Sprinkle with toasted almonds, if desired.

Cook's Tip
Skin frozen fish when it is only partially thawed. Slide the tip of a knife under the skin to loosen, grip it firmly and pull it off.

Hot Spicy Shrimp with Campanelle

Marinated shrimp and grilled turkey bacon make this pasta dish a treat that's hard to beat.

Serves 4–6

8 ounces cooked tiger shrimp, peeled
1–2 garlic cloves, crushed
finely grated zest of 1 lemon
1 tablespoon lemon juice
¼ teaspoon red chili paste or a large pinch of dried ground chile
1 tablespoon light soy sauce
5 ounces smoked turkey bacon
8 ounces dried campanelle
2 shallots, finely chopped
6 tablespoons white wine
¼ cup fish stock
4 firm ripe tomatoes, peeled, seeded and chopped
2 tablespoons chopped fresh parsley
salt and freshly ground black pepper

1 In a nonmetallic bowl, mix the shrimp with the garlic, lemon zest and juice, chili paste or ground chile and soy sauce. Season to taste with salt and pepper, cover and set aside to marinate for at least 1 hour.

2 Meanwhile, broil the turkey bacon under a preheated medium broiler for 3–4 minutes. Drain them on paper towels, then dice them.

3 Bring a large pan of lightly salted water to a boil and cook the pasta until *al dente*.

4 Meanwhile, put the shallots and wine in a large pan and bring to a boil over medium heat, then simmer until the shallots are soft and only about half of the wine remains.

5 Add the shrimp, together with their marinade, and bring to a boil over high heat. Stir in the smoked turkey and fish stock. Heat through for 1 minute.

6 Drain the pasta and add it to the pan with the chopped tomatoes and parsley. Toss thoroughly, transfer to a warmed bowl and serve immediately.

Mixed Summer Pasta

A pretty sauce with plenty of flavor makes this a perfect dish for dinner on a warm summer evening.

Serves 4
4 ounces green beans, cut into
   1-inch pieces
12 ounces dried fusilli lunghi
1 tablespoon olive oil
½ fennel bulb, sliced
1 bunch scallions, sliced diagonally
4 ounces yellow cherry tomatoes
4 ounces red cherry tomatoes
2 tablespoons chopped fresh dill
8 ounces cooked peeled shrimp
1 tablespoon lemon juice
1 tablespoon whole-grain mustard
¼ cup very low-fat fromage frais
salt and freshly ground
   black pepper
fresh dill sprigs, to garnish

1 Bring a large pan of lightly salted water to a boil and cook the beans for 5 minutes, until tender. Lift out with a slotted spoon, refresh under cold water and drain again. Set aside.

2 Bring the water back to a boil, add the pasta and cook until it is *al dente*.

3 Meanwhile, heat the oil in a large nonstick frying pan. Add the fennel and scallions, and sauté, stirring occasionally, for about 5 minutes.

4 Stir in the cherry tomatoes and cook for 5 more minutes, stirring occasionally.

5 Add the dill and shrimp to the pan, cook for 1 minute, then stir in the lemon juice, mustard, fromage frais and beans. Season to taste and simmer for 1 minute.

6 Drain the pasta and add it to the shrimp and vegetable sauce. Toss well. Serve immediately, garnished with the fresh dill.

Saffron & Seafood Pappardelle

This resembles a Breton fish stew, and the broad ribbons of tender pasta are a welcome bonus.

Serves 4
a large pinch of saffron threads
4 sun-dried tomatoes, chopped
1 teaspoon fresh thyme
¼ cup hot water
8 ounces baby squid
8 ounces monkfish fillet
2–3 garlic cloves, crushed
2 small onions, quartered
1 small fennel bulb, trimmed
   and sliced
⅔ cup white wine
12 large shrimp in their shells
8 ounces fresh pappardelle
salt and freshly ground
   black pepper
2 tablespoons chopped fresh
   parsley, to garnish

1 Put the saffron, sun-dried tomatoes and thyme into a bowl. Pour in the hot water. Let soak for 30 minutes.

2 Pull the head from the body of each squid and remove the quill. Cut the tentacles from the head and rinse these under cold water. Pull off the outer skin, then cut the body into ¼-inch rings. Cut the monkfish into 1-inch cubes.

3 Bring a large pan of lightly salted water to a boil. Put the garlic, onions and fennel into a separate pan and pour in the wine. Cover and simmer for 5 minutes, until tender.

4 Add the monkfish to the onion mixture, then pour in the sun-dried tomato mixture. Cover and cook for 3 minutes, then add the shrimp in their shells and squid. Cover and cook over low heat for 1–2 minutes. Do not overcook or the squid will toughen. Season to taste with salt and pepper.

5 Meanwhile, add the pasta to the pan of boiling water and cook until *al dente*.

6 Drain the pasta, divide it among four warmed dishes and top with the fish and shellfish sauce. Sprinkle with the chopped parsley and serve immediately.

Seafood Conchiglione with Spinach

Conchiglione are very large pasta shells, measuring about 1½ inches; don't try stuffing smaller shells—it's much too hard!

Serves 4

32 conchiglione
2 tablespoons low-fat spread, plus extra for greasing
8 scallions, finely sliced
6 tomatoes, peeled and chopped
1 cup low-fat cream cheese
6 tablespoons skimmed milk
pinch of freshly grated nutmeg
8 ounces cooked peeled shrimp
6-ounce can white crabmeat, drained and flaked
4 ounces frozen chopped spinach, thawed and drained
salt and freshly ground black pepper

1 Preheat the oven to 300°F. Bring a large pan of lightly salted water to a boil and cook the conchiglione for 10 minutes. Drain, rinse with boiling water, then drain again.

2 Melt the butter in a small saucepan. Add the scallions and cook over low heat, stirring occasionally, for 3–4 minutes or until softened. Stir in the tomatoes and cook for another 4–5 minutes.

3 Put the cream cheese and milk in a saucepan and heat gently, stirring until blended. Season to taste with salt, pepper and a pinch of nutmeg. Spoon 2 tablespoons of the cheese sauce into a bowl and set the remainder aside.

4 Add the scallion and tomato mixture to the sauce in the bowl, together with the shrimp and flaked crabmeat. Mix thoroughly.

5 Spoon the seafood filling into the pasta shells and place in a single layer in a lightly greased shallow ovenproof dish. Cover with aluminum foil and bake for 10 minutes.

6 Stir the spinach into the remaining cheese sauce. Bring to a boil, then simmer gently for 1 minute, stirring constantly. Drizzle on the filled conchiglione and serve hot.

Baked Seafood Pasta

So simple to make it's bound to become a family favorite, this is a wonderful way of serving pasta.

Serves 6

5 tablespoons low-fat spread, plus extra for greasing
8 ounces dried fettuccine
¼ cup all-purpose flour
2 cups skimmed milk
½ teaspoon dried mustard
1 teaspoon lemon juice
1 tablespoon tomato paste
½ onion, finely chopped
2 celery stalks, diced
1¼ cups small mushrooms, sliced
8 ounces cooked peeled shrimp
8 ounces crabmeat
1 tablespoon chopped fresh dill
salt and freshly ground black pepper
fresh dill sprigs, to garnish

1 Preheat the oven to 350°F. Generously grease a large ovenproof dish with low-fat spread.

2 Bring a large pan of lightly salted water to a boil and cook the pasta until it is *al dente*.

3 Meanwhile, melt 3 tablespoons of the low-fat spread in a saucepan. Stir in the flour and cook for 1 minute, stirring constantly, then gradually add the milk, stirring until the sauce boils and thickens.

4 Add the mustard, lemon juice and tomato paste to the sauce, and mix well. Season to taste with salt and pepper.

5 Melt the remaining low-fat spread in a frying pan. Add the onion, celery and mushrooms. Cook over medium heat, stirring occasionally, for about 5 minutes, until softened.

6 Drain the pasta and transfer it to a large mixing bowl. Add the sauce, vegetable mixture, shrimp, crabmeat and chopped dill. Stir thoroughly.

7 Pour the mixture evenly into the prepared dish. Bake for 30–40 minutes, until the top is lightly browned. Garnish with the dill sprigs and serve immediately.

Pasta with Scallops in Warm Green Tartar Sauce

When you are trying not to eat too much fat, sauces can be the thing you miss most. Here is a deliciously creamy dish that won't compromise your conscience.

Serves 4

12 large scallops
12 ounces dried black tagliatelle
¼ cup white wine
⅔ cup fish stock
lime wedges and parsley sprigs, to garnish

For the tartar sauce

½ cup low-fat crème fraîche
2 teaspoons whole-grain mustard
2 garlic cloves, crushed
2–3 tablespoons freshly squeezed lime juice
¼ cup chopped fresh parsley
2 tablespoons snipped chives
salt and freshly ground black pepper

1 Slice the scallops in half, horizontally. Keep any corals whole. Set aside.

2 To make the tartar sauce, mix the crème fraîche, mustard, garlic, lime juice and herbs in a bowl. Season with salt and pepper to taste.

3 Bring a large pan of lightly salted water to a boil and cook the pasta until it is *al dente*.

4 Meanwhile, put the white wine and fish stock into a pan. Heat to the simmering point. Add the scallops and cook very gently for 3–4 minutes (no longer, or they will become tough).

5 Lift out the scallops with a slotted spoon. Boil the wine and stock to reduce by half, then add the tartar sauce to the pan. Heat gently, replace the scallops and cook for 1 minute.

6 Drain the pasta and divide it among four warmed bowls. Spoon on the scallops and sauce, garnish with lime wedges and parsley, and serve.

Devilled Crab Conchiglione

Large pasta shells are perfect for stuffing, and this is a really tasty filling.

Serves 4

3 cups dried conchiglione
scant 1 cup low-fat cream cheese
⅔ cup skim milk
½ teaspoon ground paprika
1 teaspoon Dijon mustard
1 tablespoon dried bread crumbs
2 teaspoons freshly grated Parmesan cheese

For the filling

1 shallot, finely chopped
1 celery stalk, finely chopped
½ small red bell pepper, seeded and finely chopped
3 tablespoons white wine
3 tablespoons low-fat crème fraîche
2 6-ounce cans crabmeat in water, drained
3 tablespoons fresh white bread crumbs
2 tablespoons freshly grated Parmesan cheese
1 tablespoon Dijon mustard
½ teaspoon red chili paste
salt and freshly ground black pepper

1 To make the filling, put the shallot, celery, red pepper and wine into a small pan, cover and cook gently for 3–4 minutes, until the vegetables are tender and little of the wine remains. Remove the pan from heat and stir in the crème fraîche, crabmeat, fresh bread crumbs, Parmesan, mustard and chili paste. Season, if necessary.

2 Bring a large pan of lightly salted water to a boil and cook the conchiglione, in batches if necessary, until *al dente*. Drain well, then arrange upside down on a clean dish towel to dry.

3 Put the cream cheese, milk, paprika and mustard into a small pan. Heat gently and whisk until smooth. Season to taste. Pour the sauce into a large ovenproof dish.

4 Preheat the oven to 425°F. Fill the conchiglione with the crab mixture, and arrange them on top of the sauce. Mix the dried bread crumbs and Parmesan, and sprinkle on top. Cover the dish with aluminum foil and bake for 15 minutes. Uncover and return to the oven for 5 more minutes. Serve immediately.

Black Pasta with Vegetables

Black pasta derives its color from the addition of squid ink and looks very dramatic with the colorful vegetables. The avocado will push up the fat content, so leave it out if you prefer.

Serves 4

3 garlic cloves, crushed
1 tablespoon white
    tarragon vinegar
1 teaspoon Dijon mustard
2 tablespoons extra virgin olive oil

1 teaspoon finely chopped
    fresh thyme
1 yellow bell pepper, seeded
1 red bell pepper, seeded
8 ounces snow peas, trimmed
6 radishes
4 ripe plum tomatoes, peeled
    and seeded
1/2 avocado (optional)
10 ounces dried black pasta
salt and freshly ground
    black pepper
12 fresh basil leaves, to garnish

1 Make a dressing by whisking the garlic, vinegar, mustard, olive oil and chopped thyme together in a large bowl. Season to taste with salt and black pepper.

2 Cut the red and yellow peppers into diamond shapes, halve the snow peas and slice the radishes.

3 Dice the tomatoes. Peel, pit and slice the avocado, if using. Place all the vegetables in a bowl and add the dressing, stirring thoroughly to mix.

4 Bring a large pan of lightly salted water to a boil and cook the pasta until *al dente*.

5 Drain and put the pasta in a large shallow serving dish. Cover with the dressed vegetables and serve immediately, garnished with basil leaves.

> **Variation**
> *Instead of black pasta, you could use Japanese soba or buckwheat noodles, which have a nutty flavor and texture.*

Spaghetti with White Clam Sauce

This is a low-fat version of one of Italy's most famous pasta dishes.

Serves 4

2 1/4 pounds fresh clams
1/2 cup dry white wine
12 ounces dried spaghetti

2 tablespoons olive oil
2 whole garlic cloves, peeled
3 tablespoons chopped fresh
    flat-leaf parsley
salt and freshly ground
    black pepper

1 Scrub the clams under cold running water, discarding any that are open or that do not close when sharply tapped against the work surface.

2 Put the clams in a large pan, add the wine, then cover the pan tightly and place it over high heat. Cook, shaking the pan frequently, for about 5 minutes, until the clams are opened.

3 Using a slotted spoon, transfer the clams to a bowl, discarding any that have failed to open. Strain the liquid and set it aside. Put 12 clams in their shells to one side for the garnish, then remove the rest from their shells.

4 Bring a large pan of lightly salted water to a boil and cook the pasta until it is *al dente*.

5 Meanwhile, heat the oil in a deep pan. Fry the whole garlic cloves over medium heat until golden, crushing them with the back of a spoon. Remove the garlic with a slotted spoon and discard.

6 Add the shelled clams to the garlic-flavored oil and moisten them with some of the strained liquid from the clams. Season with plenty of pepper. Cook for 1–2 minutes, gradually adding more liquid as the sauce reduces. Stir in the parsley and cook for another 1–2 minutes.

7 Drain the pasta, add it to the pan and toss well. Serve in individual dishes, garnished with the reserved clams.

Trenette with Shellfish

Colorful and delicious, this is ideal for a dinner party.

Serves 4
2 tablespoons olive oil
1 small onion, finely chopped
1 garlic clove, crushed
1/2 fresh red chile, seeded and chopped
7-ounce can chopped tomatoes
2 tablespoons chopped fresh parsley

14 ounces live clams, scrubbed
14 ounces live mussels, scrubbed and bearded
1/4 cup dry white wine
3 1/2 cups dried trenette
a few fresh basil leaves
3 1/2 ounces cooked peeled shrimp
salt and freshly ground black pepper
chopped fresh herbs, to garnish

1 Heat 2 tablespoons of the oil in a saucepan and cook the onion, garlic and chile for 1–2 minutes. Stir in the tomatoes, half the parsley and pepper to taste. Bring to a boil, lower the heat, cover and simmer for 15 minutes.

2 Discard any shellfish that are open or that do not close when sharply tapped against the work surface. Heat the remaining oil in a large saucepan. Add the clams and mussels, with the rest of the parsley and toss over high heat for a few seconds.

3 Pour in the wine, then cover tightly. Cook for 5 minutes, shaking the pan frequently, until the clams and mussels have opened. Using a slotted spoon, transfer them to a bowl, discarding any shellfish that have failed to open.

4 Strain the cooking liquid and set aside. Reserve some clams and mussels, then shell the rest. Bring a large pan of lightly salted water to a boil and cook the pasta until it is *al dente*.

5 Meanwhile, add 1/2 cup of the reserved seafood liquid to the tomato sauce. Bring to a boil, lower the heat, tear in the basil leaves and stir in the shrimp and shellfish.

6 Drain the pasta and transfer it to a warmed bowl. Add the seafood sauce and toss well. Serve in warmed bowls. Sprinkle each portion with herbs and garnish with the reserved shellfish.

Tagliolini with Mussels & Clams

This makes a stunning appetizer for a dinner party.

Serves 4
1 pound fresh clams, scrubbed
1 pound fresh mussels, scrubbed and bearded
2 tablespoons olive oil
1 small onion, finely chopped
2 garlic cloves, finely chopped
1 large handful fresh flat-leaf parsley, plus extra chopped parsley to garnish

3/4 cup dry white wine
1 cup fish stock
1 small fresh red chile, seeded and chopped
12 ounces dried squid ink tagliolini
salt and freshly ground black pepper

1 Check the clams and mussels, and discard any that are open or that fail to close when tapped on the work surface.

2 Heat half the oil in a saucepan and cook the onion until soft. Add the garlic, half the parsley and seasoning. Add the clams, mussels and wine, cover and bring to a boil. Cook for 5 minutes, shaking the pan frequently, until the shellfish have opened.

3 Drain the shellfish in a fine sieve set over a bowl. Discard the aromatics, with any shellfish that have failed to open. Return the strained liquid to the clean pan and add the stock. Chop the remaining parsley finely; add it to the pan with the chile. Bring to a boil, then simmer, until slightly reduced. Turn off the heat.

4 Remove and discard the top shells from about half the clams and mussels. Put all the clams and mussels in the pan of liquid and seasonings, then cover the pan tightly and set aside.

5 Bring a large pan of lightly salted water to a boil and cook the pasta until *al dente*. Drain it, return it to the clean pan and toss with the remaining olive oil. Put the pan of shellfish over high heat and toss to heat through. Divide the pasta among four warmed plates, spoon on the shellfish mixture, sprinkle with the extra parsley and serve.

Spaghetti Marinara

Shrimps and clams combine to make a superb seafood sauce which can be used with any type of pasta.

Serves 4

1 tablespoon olive oil
1 medium onion, chopped
1 garlic clove, finely chopped
8 ounces dried spaghetti
2 1/2 cups passata
1 tablespoon tomato paste
1 teaspoon dried oregano
1 bay leaf
1 teaspoon sugar
2 cups cooked peeled shrimp
1 1/2 cups cooked clams or
  cockles, rinsed well if canned
  or bottled
1 tablespoon lemon juice
3 tablespoons chopped
  fresh parsley
1 tablespoon butter
salt and freshly ground
  black pepper

1 Heat the oil in a large saucepan and add the onion and garlic. Sauté over medium heat, stirring occasionally, for 6–7 minutes, until the onion has softened.

2 Bring a large saucepan of lightly salted water to a boil and cook the spaghetti until *al dente*.

3 Meanwhile, stir the passata, tomato paste, oregano, bay leaf and sugar into the onions, and season to taste with salt and pepper. Bring to a boil, then lower the heat and simmer for 2–3 minutes.

4 Add the shrimps, clams or cockles, lemon juice and 2 tablespoons of the parsley to the passata mixture. Stir well, then cover and cook for 6–7 minutes.

5 Drain the spaghetti. Melt the butter in the clean pan. Return the drained pasta to the pan and toss with the butter. Season to taste with salt and pepper.

6 Divide the spaghetti among four warmed plates and top with the seafood sauce. Sprinkle with the remaining parsley and serve immediately.

Baked Seafood Spaghetti

Good things come in small packages, and in this case parchment parcels are opened at the table to reveal a tasty seafood and pasta filling.

Serves 4

1 pound live mussels, scrubbed
  and bearded
1/2 cup dry white wine
2 tablespoons olive oil
2 garlic cloves, finely chopped
1 pound tomatoes, peeled and
  finely chopped
14 ounces dried spaghetti or
  other long pasta
8 ounces cooked peeled shrimp
2 tablespoons chopped
  fresh parsley
salt and freshly ground
  black pepper

1 Check the mussels, discarding any that are not tightly closed or that fail to close when tapped on the work surface. Put them in a large pan with the wine. Cover the pan and place it over medium heat. As soon as the mussels open, lift them out with a slotted spoon. Discard any that remain closed.

2 Pour the cooking liquid through a strainer lined with paper towels, and reserve. Preheat the oven to 300°F.

3 Heat the oil in a medium saucepan and cook the garlic for 1–2 minutes. Add the tomatoes and cook until they soften. Stir in ¾ cup of the cooking liquid from the mussels.

4 Bring a large pan of lightly salted water to a boil. Add the spaghetti and cook until it is *al dente*.

5 When the pasta is almost cooked, add the shrimp and parsley to the tomato sauce. Season and remove from heat. Drain the pasta and mix it with the sauce and mussels.

6 Cut out four 18 x 12-inch pieces of nonstick baking parchment. Divide the pasta and seafood mixture among them and twist the paper ends together to make a sealed package. Arrange in a roasting pan and bake for 8–10 minutes. Place one unopened package on each plate and serve.

Spaghetti with Clams

Clams, especially the hard-shell varieties and ocean quahogs, are particularly popular on the Atlantic seaboard, which is where this version of the well-known dish originated.

Serves 4

24 live clams, in their
   shells, scrubbed

I cup water
$^{1}/_{2}$ cup dry white wine
I pound dried spaghetti
I tablespoon olive oil
2 garlic cloves, finely chopped
3 tablespoons finely chopped
   fresh parsley
salt and freshly ground
   black pepper

I Rinse the clams well in cold water and drain. Discard any that are open and do not shut when sharply tapped on a work surface. Place the clams in a large pan with the measured water and wine. Bring to a boil, cover and steam, shaking the pan frequently, for 6–8 minutes or until the shells open.

2 Discard any clams that have not opened. Remove the rest from their shells. Cut off and discard the siphon from any large clams and roughly chop the flesh.

3 Pour the cooking liquid through a strainer lined with paper towels. Place in a small saucepan and boil rapidly until it has reduced by about half. Set aside.

4 Bring a large pan of lightly salted water to a boil. Add the spaghetti and cook until it is al dente.

5 Meanwhile, heat the olive oil in a large frying pan. Add the garlic and cook for 2–3 minutes, but do not let it brown. Add the reduced clam liquid and the parsley. Let it cook over low heat until the spaghetti is ready.

6 Drain the spaghetti. Add it to the frying pan, raise the heat to medium, and add the clams. Cook for 3–4 minutes, tossing the pasta with the sauce. Season to taste with salt and pepper, and serve immediately.

Linguine with Clam & Tomato Sauce

Simple and supremely satisfying, this classic Italian dish is low in fat, so will suit those who are watching their diet.

Serves 4

2 pounds live clams in their
   shells, scrubbed
I cup water

12 ounces dried linguine
I tablespoon olive oil
I garlic clove, crushed
14 ounces tomatoes, fresh or
   canned, very finely chopped
$^{1}/_{4}$ cup chopped fresh parsley
salt and freshly ground
   black pepper

I Rinse the clams well in cold water and drain. Discard any that are open and do not shut when sharply tapped on a work surface. Place them in a large saucepan with the measured water. Bring to a boil, cover and steam for 6–8 minutes, until the shells open. Lift out the clams with a slotted spoon, discarding any that remain shut.

2 Remove the clams from their shells, adding any juices to the liquid in the pan. Cut off and discard the siphon from any large clams and chop the flesh into two or three pieces. Strain the cooking juices through a sieve lined with paper towels.

3 Bring a large pan of lightly salted water to a boil and cook the pasta until it is al dente. Meanwhile, heat the olive oil in a separate pan. Add the garlic and cook over medium heat until the garlic is golden, then discard it.

4 Add the chopped tomatoes to the oil, and pour in the clam cooking liquid. Mix well and cook until the sauce begins to dry out and thicken slightly.

5 Stir the parsley and clams into the tomato sauce and increase the heat. Season to taste with pepper. Drain the pasta and put it in a warmed serving bowl. Pour on the hot sauce and mix well before serving.

Soba Noodles with Nori

Tender noodles, crisp toasted seaweed and a savory dipping sauce make for a simple, but delicious light meal.

Serves 4
12 ounces dried soba noodles
1 sheet nori seaweed

For the dipping sauce
1 1/4 cups bonito stock
1/2 cup dark soy sauce
1/4 cup mirin
1 teaspoon sugar
1/4 ounce loose bonito flakes

For the flavorings
4 scallions, finely chopped
2 tablespoons grated daikon
wasabi paste

1 Make the dipping sauce. Combine the stock, soy sauce, mirin and sugar in a saucepan. Bring rapidly to a boil, add the bonito flakes, then remove from heat. When cool, strain the sauce into a bowl and cover.

2 Bring a pan of lightly salted water to a boil and cook the soba noodles for 6–7 minutes or until just tender, following the manufacturer's directions on the package.

3 Drain the noodles and then rinse them under cold running water, agitating them gently to remove the excess starch. Drain well again.

4 Toast the nori over high heat or under a preheated broiler, then crumble into thin strips. Divide the noodles among four serving dishes and top with the nori. Serve each portion with an individual bowl of dipping sauce and pass the flavorings separately.

Cook's Tip
The dipping sauce can be made up to a week before it is needed. Cover it and keep it in the refrigerator.

Egg Noodles with Tuna & Tomato Sauce

Raid the pantry, add a few fresh ingredients and you can produce a scrumptious main meal in a matter of moments.

Serves 4
1 tablespoon olive oil
2 garlic cloves, finely chopped
2 dried red chiles, seeded and chopped
1 large red onion, thinly sliced
6-ounce can tuna in water, drained
6–8 pitted black olives
14-ounce can chopped tomatoes
2 tablespoons chopped fresh parsley
12 ounces medium-thick dried egg noodles
salt and freshly ground black pepper

1 Heat the oil in a large frying pan. Add the garlic and dried chiles, and sauté for a few seconds, then add the sliced onion. Cook over medium heat, stirring occasionally, for about 5 minutes, until the onion softens.

2 Add the tuna and olives to the pan, and stir until well mixed. Stir in the tomatoes, with any juices. Bring to a boil, season well, stir in the parsley, then lower the heat and simmer gently.

3 Meanwhile, bring a large pan of lightly salted water to a boil. Add the noodles and cook them until just tender, following the directions on the package.

4 Drain the noodles well and return them to the clean pan. Add the sauce, toss to mix and serve immediately.

Cook's Tip
Depending on the contents of your pantry, you could substitute other canned fish for the tuna. Try mackerel, sardines or salmon, for example. You could also add bottled clams or canned anchovies.

Seafood & Vermicelli Stir-fry

Seafood is the perfect choice for stir-fries, as it requires the fastest of cooking and combines superbly with noodles.

Serves 4

1 pound rice vermicelli, soaked in warm water until soft
1 tablespoon vegetable oil
½ cup drained sun-dried tomatoes, reconstituted in water then drained and sliced
3 scallions, sliced on the diagonal
2 large carrots, cut into batons
1 zucchini, cut into batons
8 ounces shrimp, peeled and deveined
8 ounces shelled scallops
1-inch piece of fresh ginger root, finely grated
3 tablespoons lemon juice
3 tablespoons chopped fresh basil
salt and freshly ground black pepper

1 Bring a large pan of lightly salted water to a boil. Add the rice vermicelli and cook until tender, following the instructions on the package. Drain, rinse with boiling water, and drain again thoroughly. Keep warm.

2 Heat a wok, add the oil, then stir-fry the sun-dried tomatoes, scallions and carrots over high heat for 5 minutes.

3 Add the zucchini, shrimp, scallops and ginger. Stir-fry for 3 minutes.

4 Pour in the lemon juice. Add the basil, with salt and pepper to taste, and stir well. Stir-fry for 2 more minutes. Divide the rice vermicelli among individual plates and spoon the stir-fried mixture on top. Serve immediately.

Cook's Tip
The easiest way to prepare the carrots and zucchini is to slice them lengthwise, then cut them across in thin sticks. Don't make them matchstick-thin or they will overcook.

Buckwheat Noodles with Smoked Trout

The light, crisp texture of the bok choy balances the tender shiitake mushrooms and noodles and perfectly complements the delicate flesh of smoked trout.

Serves 4

12 ounces buckwheat or soba noodles
1 tablespoon vegetable oil
4 ounces fresh shiitake mushrooms, quartered
2 garlic cloves, finely chopped
1 tablespoon grated fresh ginger root
8 ounces bok choy, trimmed and separated into leaves
1 scallion, finely sliced on the diagonal
1 teaspoon dark sesame oil
2 tablespoons mirin or dry sherry
2 tablespoons soy sauce
2 smoked trout, skinned and boned
salt
2 tablespoons cilantro leaves and 2 teaspoons toasted sesame seeds, to garnish

1 Bring a large pan of lightly salted water to a boil and cook the buckwheat or soba noodles until just tender, following the instructions on the package.

2 Meanwhile, heat a wok until hot, add the oil and swirl it around. Add the shiitake mushrooms and stir-fry over medium heat for 3 minutes.

3 Add the garlic, ginger and bok choy and toss over the heat for another 2 minutes.

4 Drain the noodles very well and add them to the mushroom mixture, together with the scallions, sesame oil, mirin or sherry and soy sauce. Stir briefly until heated through.

5 Break the smoked trout into bite-size pieces. Arrange the noodle mixture on individual serving plates. Place the smoked trout on top, garnish with cilantro leaves and sesame seeds, and serve immediately.

Noodles with Shrimp in Lemon Sauce

In this Chinese dish, it is the noodles that are the prime ingredient, with seafood playing a minor, but still important, role in terms of flavor and color.

Serves 4

2 packages dried egg noodles
1 tablespoon sunflower oil
2 celery stalks, cut
   into matchsticks
2 garlic cloves, crushed
4 scallions, sliced

2 carrots, cut into matchsticks
3-inch piece of cucumber, cut
   into matchsticks
4 ounces shrimp, in their shells
pared zest and juice of 1 lemon
1 teaspoon cornstarch
4–5 tablespoons fish stock
1 cup cooked peeled shrimp
salt and freshly ground
   black pepper
fresh dill sprigs, to garnish

1 Bring a large pan of lightly salted water to a boil and cook the noodles until tender.

2 Meanwhile, heat the oil in a pan and stir-fry the celery, garlic, scallions and carrots for 2–3 minutes. Add the cucumber and shell-on shrimp, and cook for 2–3 minutes. Blanch the pared lemon zest in boiling water for 1 minute.

3 Mix the lemon juice with the cornstarch and stock, and add to the pan. Bring gently to a boil, stirring, and cook for 1 minute.

4 Drain the lemon zest and add it to the pan, with the peeled shrimp. Season to taste. Drain the noodles and serve with the shrimp sauce. Garnish each portion with dill.

Cook's Tip
Dried egg noodles need very little cooking. In some cases you just immerse them in boiling water for a few minutes. Always check the instructions on the package.

Chili Squid & Noodles

In China, this popular noodle dish is traditionally cooked in a clay pot.

Serves 4

1½ pounds prepared squid
1 tablespoon vegetable oil
3 slices of fresh ginger root,
   finely shredded
2 garlic cloves, finely chopped
1 red onion, thinly sliced
1 carrot, thinly sliced
1 celery stalk, sliced
⅓ cup sugar snap peas, trimmed
1 teaspoon sugar

1 tablespoon chili bean paste
½ teaspoon chili powder
3 ounces cellophane noodles,
   soaked in warm water until soft
½ cup light chicken stock
1 tablespoon soy sauce
1 tablespoon oyster sauce
1 teaspoon sesame oil
salt
cilantro leaves, to garnish

1 Cut the body of the squid into rings or split it open lengthwise, score criss-cross patterns on the inside of the body and cut it into 2 x 1½-inch pieces.

2 Heat the oil in a flameproof casserole. Add the ginger, garlic and onion, and sauté, stirring occasionally, for 1–2 minutes.

3 Add the squid, carrot, celery and sugar snap peas. Cook until the squid curls up. Season with salt to taste and stir in the sugar, chili bean paste and chili powder. Transfer the mixture to a bowl and set aside.

4 Drain the soaked noodles and add them to the casserole. Stir in the stock and sauces. Cover and cook for 10 minutes or until the noodles are tender.

5 Return the squid and vegetables to the casserole. Cover and cook for 5–6 more minutes, until all the flavors are combined. Serve in warmed bowls.

6 Drizzle each portion with sesame oil and sprinkle with the cilantro leaves.

Sweet-and-Sour Shrimp with Noodles

Chinese dried noodles need very little cooking. Use one skein per person.

Serves 4–6
1/4 cup Chinese dried mushrooms
1 1/4 cups hot water
1 bunch of scallions, cut into thick
   diagonal slices
1-inch piece fresh ginger
   root, grated
1 red bell pepper, seeded
   and diced
8-ounce can water chestnuts, sliced
3 tablespoons light soy sauce
2 tablespoons sherry
12 ounces large cooked
   peeled shrimp
8 ounces dried egg noodles

1 Put the Chinese dried mushrooms into a bowl. Pour over the measured hot water and set aside to soak for 15 minutes.

2 Strain the soaking liquid through a fine sieve into a pan. Chop the mushrooms and add them to the pan, with the scallions, ginger and diced red pepper. Bring to a boil, lower the heat, cover and cook for about 5 minutes, until the vegetables are tender.

3 Add the water chestnuts, soy sauce, sherry and shrimp to the vegetable mixture. Cover and cook gently for 2 minutes.

4 Meanwhile, bring a large pan of lightly salted water to a boil. Add the noodles and cook them until just tender, checking the package for information on timing. Drain thoroughly and put into a warmed serving dish. Spoon the sweet-and-sour shrimp on top and toss to mix. Serve immediately.

Cook's Tip
The Chinese vegetable water chestnuts (ma taai) are small corms with crisp white flesh and dark brown skins. They are sometimes available fresh and should be carefully peeled before use. Confusingly, there is a Chinese nut also known as the water chestnut (ling gok), but this is quite different.

Spicy Singapore Noodles

A delicious dinner dish with a stunning mix of flavors and textures, as well as a hint of spiciness.

Serves 4
8 ounces dried egg noodles
1 tablespoon peanut oil
1 onion, chopped
1-inch piece fresh ginger root,
   finely chopped
1 garlic clove, finely chopped
1 tablespoon Madras
   curry powder
4 ounces cooked chicken or pork,
   finely shredded
4 ounces cooked peeled shrimp
4 ounces Chinese cabbage
   leaves, shredded
2 cups bean sprouts
1/4 cup defatted chicken stock
1–2 tablespoons dark soy sauce
salt
1–2 fresh red chiles, seeded and
   finely shredded and 4 scallions,
   finely shredded, to garnish

1 Bring a large pan of lightly salted water to a boil and cook the noodles until they are just tender, checking the package for information on timing.

2 Rinse the noodles thoroughly under cold water and drain well. Add 1 teaspoon of the oil, toss lightly and set aside.

3 Preheat a wok and swirl in the remaining oil. When it is hot, add the onion, ginger and garlic, and stir-fry over medium heat for about 2 minutes.

4 Stir in the curry powder and 1/2 teaspoon salt, stir-fry for 30 seconds, then add the drained noodles, chicken or pork and shrimp. Stir-fry for 3–4 minutes.

5 Add the shredded Chinese cabbage and bean sprouts, and stir-fry for 1–2 more minutes. Sprinkle in the stock and soy sauce to taste, and toss well until evenly mixed and heated through. Divide among warmed individual serving bowls or plates, garnish with the shredded red chiles and scallions, and serve immediately.

POULTRY &
MEAT

Orecchiette with Bacon & Chicken Livers

Sherry balances the saltiness of the bacon in this superbly rich sauce.

Serves 4

3 cups dried orecchiette
8 ounces frozen chicken livers,
    thawed and drained
1 tablespoon olive oil
6 ounces lean bacon,
    roughly chopped
2 garlic cloves, crushed
14-ounce can chopped tomatoes
²/₃ cup chicken stock
1 tablespoon tomato paste
1 tablespoon dry sherry
2 tablespoons chopped
    mixed fresh herbs
salt and freshly ground
    black pepper
freshly grated Parmesan
    cheese, to serve (optional)

1 Bring a large pan of lightly salted water to a boil and cook the pasta until it is *al dente*.

2 Meanwhile, trim the chicken livers and cut them into bite-size pieces. Heat the olive oil in a sauté pan, add the bacon and fry for 3–4 minutes.

3 Add the garlic and chicken livers to the pan and fry for another 2–3 minutes. Stir in the tomatoes, chicken stock, tomato paste, sherry and herbs, and season with salt and pepper.

4 Bring to a boil, then lower the heat and simmer gently, uncovered, for about 5 minutes, until the sauce has thickened.

5 Drain the pasta, return it to the clean pan and toss it with the sauce. Serve hot, sprinkled with Parmesan cheese, if using.

Variation
You could substitute smoked or unsmoked pancetta for the bacon, if you prefer.

Tagliatelle with Chicken & Vermouth

Vermouth gives this chicken sauce a delicious flavor, with the fromage frais taking the edge off the acidity.

Serves 4

1 tablespoon olive oil
1 red onion, cut into wedges
12 ounces dried tagliatelle
1 garlic clove, chopped
12 ounces skinless, boneless
    chicken breasts, diced
1¹/₄ cups dry vermouth
3 tablespoons chopped
    mixed fresh herbs
²/₃ cup very-low-fat fromage frais
salt and freshly ground
    black pepper
shredded fresh mint, to garnish

1 Heat the oil in a large heavy frying pan. Add the onion and sauté for about 10 minutes, until it starts to soften and the layers separate.

2 Bring a large pan of lightly salted water to a boil and cook the pasta until it is *al dente*.

3 Meanwhile, add the garlic and chicken to the onion and fry, stirring occasionally, for 10 minutes, until the chicken has browned all over and is cooked through.

4 Pour in the vermouth, bring to a boil and boil rapidly until reduced by about half. Stir in the herbs and fromage frais, and season with salt and pepper to taste. Heat through gently, but do not let the sauce boil.

5 Drain the pasta, return it to the clean pan and toss it with the sauce to coat. Serve in warmed bowls, garnished with the shredded mint.

Variation
If you don't want to use vermouth, use dry white wine instead. Orvieto or Frascati would be ideal.

Round Ravioli with Bolognese Sauce

Tender ravioli and a richly flavored, low-fat sauce—what more could anyone wish for?

Serves 6
1 cup low-fat cottage cheese
2 tablespoons grated
   Parmesan cheese, plus extra
   for serving
1 egg white, beaten, plus extra
   for brushing
1/4 teaspoon freshly
   grated nutmeg
1 batch of Basic Pasta Dough
all-purpose flour, for dusting
salt and freshly ground
   black pepper

For the Bolognese Sauce
1 medium onion, finely chopped
1 garlic clove, crushed
2/3 cup defatted beef stock
12 ounces ground turkey
1/2 cup red wine
2 tablespoons tomato paste
14-ounce can chopped tomatoes
1/2 teaspoon chopped
   fresh rosemary
1/4 teaspoon ground allspice

1 To make the filling, mix the cottage cheese, grated Parmesan and egg white in a bowl, add the nutmeg, and season with salt and pepper to taste.

2 Roll the pasta into thin sheets. To make the ravioli, place small amounts of filling (about 1 teaspoon) in rows on half the pasta sheets at intervals of 2 inches.

3 Brush beaten egg white around each mound of filling. Top each sheet of filled pasta with a sheet of plain pasta and press between each pocket to remove any air and seal firmly.

4 Using a fluted ravioli or pastry cutter, stamp out rounds from the filled pasta and place these on a floured dish towel to dry while you make the sauce.

5 Put the onion and garlic in a pan. Add the stock and cook over medium heat until most of it has been absorbed. Stir in the turkey and cook quickly to brown, breaking up any lumps with a fork.

6 Stir in the wine, tomato paste, chopped tomatoes, rosemary and allspice, and bring to a boil. Lower the heat and simmer, stirring occasionally, for 1 hour. Adjust the seasoning to taste.

7 Bring a large pan of lightly salted water to a boil and cook the ravioli, in batches if necessary, until *al dente*. Drain thoroughly. Serve topped with the Bolognese sauce. Pass grated Parmesan cheese separately.

Cook's Tip
If you buy steak in one piece and grind it yourself, you will be sure that it is lean. Although supermarkets often label ground beef "extra lean" or "premium quality," these terms have no legal meaning. As a general rule, the lighter the color of the beef, the more fat it contains.

Spinach Tagliarini with Chicken & Asparagus

With its delicate colors and fresh flavors, this would be a good choice for an *al fresco* dinner in early summer.

Serves 4–6
2 skinless, boneless
   chicken breasts
1 tablespoon light soy sauce
2 tablespoons sherry
2 tablespoons cornstarch
8 scallions, trimmed and cut
   diagonally into 1-inch slices
1–2 garlic cloves, crushed
needle shreds of zest of 1/2 lemon
2/3 cup defatted chicken stock
1 teaspoon sugar
2 tablespoons lemon juice
8 ounces slender asparagus
   spears, trimmed and cut in
   3-inch lengths
1 pound fresh tagliarini
salt and freshly ground
   black pepper

1 Place the chicken breasts between two sheets of plastic wrap and flatten each of them to a thickness of about 1/4 inch with a rolling pin or the flat side of a meat mallet.

2 Cut the chicken across the grain into 1-inch strips. Put these into a bowl and add the soy sauce, sherry and cornstarch, and season with plenty of salt and pepper. Toss well to coat each piece.

3 Put the chicken, scallions, garlic and lemon zest in a large nonstick frying pan. Add the stock and bring to a boil, stirring constantly, until thickened. Stir in the sugar, lemon juice and asparagus. Simmer over low heat, stirring occasionally, for 4–5 minutes, until tender.

4 Meanwhile, bring a large pan of lightly salted water to a boil and cook the pasta until *al dente*.

5 Drain the tagliarini thoroughly. Divide it among warmed serving plates, and spoon on the chicken and asparagus sauce. Serve immediately.

Penne with Spinach

If you love spinach you'll really enjoy this moist and appetizing pasta dish.

Serves 4
8 ounces fresh spinach leaves
5 ounces smoked turkey bacon
3 cups dried penne, preferably
   mixed colors
1 garlic clove, crushed
1 small onion, finely chopped
½ small red bell pepper, seeded
   and finely chopped
1 small fresh red chile, seeded
   and chopped
⅔ cup vegetable stock
3 tablespoons low-fat
   crème fraîche
2 tablespoons freshly grated
   Parmesan cheese, plus extra
   to garnish
crusty bread, to serve

1 Preheat the broiler. Wash the spinach leaves and remove the hard central stems. Shred the leaves finely and set them aside.

2 Cook the smoked turkey bacon under a preheated medium broiler for 3–4 minutes, until lightly browned. Let them cool a little, then chop them finely.

3 Bring a large pan of lightly salted water to a boil and cook the pasta until it is *al dente*.

4 Meanwhile, put the garlic, onion, red pepper and chile into a large frying pan. Pour in the stock, cover and cook for about 5 minutes or until the onion is tender. Add the prepared spinach and cook quickly for 2–3 minutes, until it has wilted.

5 Drain the pasta and return it to the clean pan. Add the spinach mixture, the crème fraîche and the grated Parmesan. Toss gently but thoroughly, then pile on warmed plates, sprinkle with the chopped turkey and top with the extra Parmesan. Serve immediately with crusty bread.

Variation
Substitute arugula for the spinach, omit the chile and add a finely chopped, peeled and seeded tomato.

Pasta Bonbons

For a special occasion, these pretty little pasta packages would be a fine choice.

Serves 4–6
1 batch of Basic Pasta Dough
all-purpose flour, for dusting
1 egg white, beaten
salt and freshly ground
   black pepper

For the filling
1 small onion, finely chopped
1 garlic clove, crushed
⅔ cup defatted chicken stock
8 ounces ground turkey
2–3 fresh sage leaves, chopped
2 drained canned anchovy fillets

For the sauce
⅔ cup defatted chicken stock
scant 1 cup low-fat
   cream cheese
1 tablespoon lemon juice
1 teaspoon sugar
2 tomatoes, peeled, seeded and
   finely diced
½ red onion, finely chopped
6 small cornichons (pickled
   gherkins), sliced

1 Make the filling. Put the onion, garlic and stock into a pan. Bring to a boil, cover and simmer for 5 minutes, until the onion is tender. Uncover and boil for about 5 minutes or until the stock has reduced to 2 tablespoons.

2 Add the ground turkey and stir it over the heat until lightly colored. Add the sage and anchovy fillets, and season to taste with salt and pepper. Cook uncovered for 5 minutes, until all the liquid has been absorbed. Let cool.

3 Divide the pasta dough in half. Roll one half into thin sheets and cut into 3½ x 2½-inch rectangles. Lay these on a lightly floured dish towel and repeat with the remaining dough.

4 Place a heaped teaspoon of the filling on the center of each rectangle, brush the surrounding dough with beaten egg white and roll up the pasta to make bonbons or small crackers, pinching in the ends. Transfer to a floured dish towel and let rest for 1 hour before cooking.

5 To make the sauce, put the stock, cream cheese, lemon juice and sugar into a pan. Heat gently and whisk until smooth. Add the diced tomatoes, onion and cornichons, and leave over low heat while you cook the bonbons.

6 Bring a large pan of lightly salted water to a boil and cook the bonbons, in batches, for 5 minutes. As each batch becomes tender, lift out the bonbons with a slotted spoon, drain well and drop into the sauce. When all the bonbons have been added, simmer them in the sauce for 2–3 minutes. Serve in warmed bowls, spooning a little sauce on each bonbon.

Cook's Tip
Allow plenty of time for making these. The bonbons need to rest for at least an hour before being cooked.

Low-fat Spaghetti alla Carbonara

Smoked turkey bacon make a good substitute for bacon in this new look at an old favorite.

Serves 4

5 ounces smoked turkey bacon
1 medium onion, chopped
1–2 garlic cloves, crushed
²/₃ cup vegetable stock or
   defatted chicken stock
1 pound chili and
   garlic-flavored spaghetti
²/₃ cup dry white wine
scant 1 cup low-fat cream cheese
2 tablespoons chopped
   fresh parsley
salt and freshly ground
   black pepper
shavings of Parmesan cheese,
   to serve

1 Cut the turkey bacon into ¹/₂-inch strips. Dry-fry in a nonstick pan over medium heat for 2–3 minutes.

2 Add the onion, garlic and stock to the pan. Bring to a boil, lower the heat, cover and simmer while you cook the pasta.

3 Bring a large pan of lightly salted water to a boil and cook the pasta until it is *al dente*.

4 Meanwhile, add the wine to the turkey mixture and bring to a boil. Boil rapidly until reduced by half.

5 Whisk the cream cheese into the turkey mixture, beating until smooth. Season to taste with salt and pepper.

6 Drain the pasta, return it to the clean pan, and add the sauce and the chopped parsley. Toss well. Serve immediately in warmed bowls, with shavings of Parmesan.

> **Cook's Tip**
> *Add the cream cheese gradually, a spoonful at a time, when making the sauce.*

Turkey & Pasta Casserole

Low in fat, turkey is a good choice for healthy family meals. Here it is combined with smoked turkey bacon, vegetables and rigatoni and topped with cheese before being baked.

Serves 4

10 ounces ground turkey
5 ounces smoked turkey
   bacon, chopped
1–2 garlic cloves, crushed
1 onion, finely chopped
2 carrots, diced
2 tablespoons tomato paste
1¹/₄ cups defatted chicken stock
2 cups dried rigatoni
2 tablespoons freshly grated
   Parmesan cheese
salt and freshly ground
   black pepper

1 Dry-fry the ground turkey in a nonstick pan over medium heat, breaking up any large pieces with a wooden spoon, until well browned all over.

2 Add the chopped turkey bacon, garlic, onion, carrots, tomato paste and stock. Bring to a boil, cover and simmer for 1 hour, until tender. Season, if necessary.

3 Preheat the oven to 350°F. Bring a large pan of lightly salted water to a boil and cook the pasta until *al dente*.

4 Drain thoroughly, return to the clean pan and mix with the turkey sauce.

5 Spoon the pasta mixture into a shallow ovenproof dish and sprinkle with the freshly grated Parmesan. Bake for 20–30 minutes. Let stand for 5 minutes before serving.

> **Cook's Tip**
> *To remove the fat from homemade chicken stock, let it cool, then chill it overnight in the refrigerator. The fat will solidify on top and will easily be lifted off.*

Spaghetti with Turkey Ragoût

Ground turkey is much lower in fat than most other meats and makes an excellent basis for a low-fat pasta meal.

Serves 4
1 pound ground turkey
1 medium onion, finely diced
1 medium carrot, diced
1 celery stalk, diced
14-ounce can chopped tomatoes
1 tablespoon tomato paste
1 teaspoon dried oregano
2 bay leaves, plus extra
   to garnish
8 ounces dried spaghetti
salt and freshly ground
   black pepper

1 In a nonstick pan, dry-fry the ground turkey with the diced onion over medium heat, stirring frequently, until the turkey is lightly colored.

2 Stir in the carrot and celery, and cook, stirring constantly, for 5–8 minutes.

3 Add the tomatoes, tomato paste, dried oregano and bay leaves. Bring to a boil, lower the heat, cover and simmer for 40 minutes, until the sauce is thick and full of flavor. Season to taste with salt and pepper.

4 Meanwhile, bring a large pan of lightly salted water to a boil and cook the spaghetti until *al dente*.

5 Drain well, divide among warmed bowls, spoon on the ragoût and serve immediately garnished with bay leaves.

Cook's tip
If you can't find ground turkey, use lean ground pork, lamb or beef and pour off all the fat from the pan before adding the vegetables.

Piquant Chicken with Spaghetti

Morsels of tender chicken in a mouthwatering sauce make this a popular dish for the whole family.

Serves 4
1 onion, finely chopped
1 carrot, diced
1 garlic clove,
   crushed
1¼ cups vegetable stock
4 small skinless, boneless
   chicken breasts
1 bouquet garni
1½ cups button mushrooms,
   thinly sliced
1 teaspoon balsamic vinegar
½ cucumber, peeled and cut
   into batons
12 ounces dried spaghetti
2 firm ripe tomatoes, peeled,
   seeded and chopped
2 tablespoons low-fat crème fraîche
1 tablespoon chopped
   fresh parsley
1 tablespoon snipped chives
salt and freshly ground
   black pepper

1 Put the onion, carrot, garlic and stock into a pan, and add the chicken breasts and bouquet garni. Bring to a boil, lower the heat, cover and simmer gently for 15–20 minutes or until tender. Transfer the chicken to a plate and cover with aluminum foil.

2 Strain the cooking liquid into a clean pan, discarding the vegetables and flavorings. Add the sliced mushrooms and balsamic vinegar, and simmer for 2–3 minutes, until tender. Using a slotted spoon, lift out the mushrooms and set them aside. Boil the stock until it is reduced by half.

3 Meanwhile, bring a large pan of lightly salted water to a boil. Add the cucumber, cook for 20 seconds, then lift out and set aside. Add the pasta to the boiling water and cook it until it is *al dente*.

4 Cut the chicken breasts into bite-size pieces and stir them into the reduced stock, with the chopped tomatoes, crème fraîche, cucumber, parsley and chives. Season with salt and pepper to taste.

5 Drain the pasta, put it in a warmed serving dish and spoon onto the piquant chicken. Serve immediately.

Rolled Stuffed Cannelloni

For tender, rustic-looking cannelloni, roll your own. Use lasagne sheets rather than rigid cannelloni tubes.

Serves 4
12 fresh or dried lasagne sheets
fresh basil leaves, to garnish

For the filling
2–3 garlic cloves, crushed
1 small onion, finely chopped
²⁄₃ cup white wine
1 pound ground turkey
1 tablespoon dried basil
1 tablespoon dried thyme
³⁄₄ cup fresh white bread crumbs

salt and freshly ground
    black pepper

For the sauce
2 tablespoons low-fat margarine
¹⁄₄ cup all-purpose flour
1¹⁄₄ cups skim milk
4 sun-dried tomatoes, soaked in
    warm water until soft, then
    drained and chopped
1 tablespoon mixed chopped
    fresh herbs
2 tablespoons freshly grated
    Parmesan cheese

1 First, make the filling. Put the garlic, onion and half the wine into a large pan. Cover and cook over low heat for 5 minutes, then increase the heat and add the turkey. Cook it quickly, breaking up any lumps with a wooden spoon, until all the liquid has evaporated.

2 Lower the heat, and add the remaining wine and the herbs. Cover and cook for 20 minutes.

3 Draw the pan off the heat, stir in the bread crumbs and season with salt and pepper to taste. Set aside to cool.

4 Bring a large pan of lightly salted water to a boil and cook the lasagne sheets, in batches if necessary, until *al dente*. Drain thoroughly, rinse in cold water and drain again. Pat dry on a clean dish towel.

5 Lay each lasagne sheet in turn on a board. Spoon turkey mixture along one short edge and roll it up to make a tube, encasing the filling. Cut the tubes in half.

6 Preheat the oven to 400°F. Make the sauce. Put the margarine, flour and skim milk into a pan, and whisk over low heat until smooth. Add the tomatoes and mixed herbs, and season to taste with salt and pepper.

7 Spoon a thin layer of the sauce into a large, shallow ovenproof dish and arrange a layer of cannelloni on top, seam side down. Spoon a layer of sauce on top, and cover with another layer of cannelloni and the remaining sauce. Sprinkle with grated Parmesan.

8 Bake for 10–15 minutes, until lightly browned. Serve immediately, garnished with fresh basil leaves.

Low-fat Lasagne

Serve this delicious lasagne with a garnish of mixed salad leaves.

Serves 6–8
1 large onion, chopped
2 garlic cloves, crushed
1¹⁄₄ pounds ground turkey
1³⁄₄ cups passata
1 teaspoon mixed dried herbs
7 ounces no-need-to-precook
    dried green lasagne sheets
scant 1 cup low-fat
    cottage cheese
8 ounces frozen leaf spinach,
    thawed and drained

For the sauce
2 tablespoons low-fat margarine
¹⁄₄ cup all-purpose flour
1¹⁄₄ cups skim milk
¹⁄₃ cup freshly grated
    Parmesan cheese
¹⁄₄ teaspoon freshly grated
    nutmeg
salt and freshly ground
    black pepper
salad greens and tomatoes,
    to serve

1 Put the onion, garlic and ground turkey into a nonstick saucepan. Cook over medium heat, stirring with a wooden spoon to break up any lumps, for 5 minutes or until the turkey is lightly browned.

2 Add the passata and dried herbs, and season with salt and pepper to taste. Bring to a boil, then lower the heat. Cover and simmer for 30 minutes.

3 To make the sauce, put the margarine, flour and skim milk in a pan and whisk constantly over low heat until the sauce boils and thickens. Stir in the Parmesan until melted. Stir in the nutmeg, and season with salt and pepper to taste.

4 Preheat the oven to 375°F. Layer the turkey mixture, lasagne sheets, cottage cheese and spinach in an ovenproof dish, starting and ending with a layer of turkey.

5 Spoon the cheese sauce evenly on top and bake for 45–50 minutes or until golden and bubbling. Let stand for 10–15 minutes before serving with salad greens and tomatoes.

Penne with Chicken & Ham Sauce

A meal in itself, this colorful pasta dish is perfect for lunch or dinner.

Serves 4

3 cups dried penne
1 tablespoon butter
1 onion, chopped
1 garlic clove, chopped
1 bay leaf
1¾ cups dry white wine
⅔ cup low-fat crème fraîche

8 ounces cooked chicken, skinned, boned and diced
4 ounces cooked lean ham, diced
½ cup grated reduced-fat Gouda cheese
1 tablespoon chopped fresh mint, plus extra to garnish
salt and freshly ground black pepper

1 Bring a pan of lightly salted water to a boil and cook the pasta until it is *al dente*.

2 Meanwhile, melt the butter in a large frying pan. Add the onion and sauté over medium heat, stirring occasionally, for 5 minutes, until softened. Add the garlic, bay leaf and wine and bring to a boil. Boil rapidly until reduced by half.

3 Remove and discard the bay leaf, then stir in the crème fraîche, chicken, ham and grated cheese. Lower the heat and simmer for 5 minutes, stirring occasionally, until heated through. Do not let the sauce boil. Stir in the chopped mint and season to taste with salt and pepper.

4 Drain the pasta and return it to the clean pan. Add the chicken and ham sauce, and toss well. Serve immediately in warmed bowls, garnished with the extra chopped mint.

- Sour cream can be used instead of crème fraîche, or use 6 tablespoons cream cheese, thinned with a little milk.
- Cooked turkey can be used instead of the chicken and prosciutto instead of ham.

Fusilli with Turkey & Roasted Tomatoes

Roasting tomatoes gives them a depth of flavor that is delicious with the pasta and broccoli.

Serves 4–6

1½ pounds ripe but firm plum tomatoes, quartered
2 tablespoons olive oil
1 teaspoon dried oregano

12 ounces broccoli florets
4 cups dried fusilli
1 small onion, sliced
1 teaspoon dried thyme
1 pound skinless, boneless turkey breast, cubed
3 garlic cloves, crushed
1 tablespoon lemon juice
salt and freshly ground black pepper

1 Preheat the oven to 400°F. Place the tomato quarters in a single layer in an ovenproof dish. Add 1 tablespoon of the olive oil, the oregano and 1 teaspoon salt, and stir to mix. Roast, without stirring, for 30–40 minutes, until the tomatoes are just browned.

2 Meanwhile, bring a large pan of lightly salted water to a boil. Add the broccoli and cook for 5 minutes, until just tender. Using a slotted spoon, transfer the broccoli to a colander, refresh it under cold water and let it drain. Reserve the pan of water.

3 Bring the reserved water back to a boil, add the pasta and cook it until it is *al dente*.

4 Meanwhile, heat the remaining oil in a large frying pan. Add the onion, thyme and turkey. Cook over high heat, stirring often, for 5–7 minutes, until the meat is cooked.

5 Add the garlic and cook for 1 more minute, stirring frequently, then stir in the lemon juice and broccoli. Season with pepper and keep hot.

6 Drain the pasta, return it to the clean pan and toss it with the sauce. Serve immediately in warmed bowls.

Pasta with Sausage, Corn & Red Bell Peppers

This Italian-American recipe cleverly combines reduced fat with all the flavor of traditional ingredients in this quick and easy dinner dish.

Serves 4

3 cups dried fusilli
  or eliche
1 tablespoon olive oil
1 onion, chopped
1 garlic clove, finely chopped
2 red bell peppers, seeded
  and sliced
1½ cups frozen corn
  kernels, thawed
1 reduced-fat U-shaped smoked
  pork sausage
1 tablespoon chopped fresh basil
salt and freshly ground
  black pepper
fresh basil sprigs, to garnish

1 Bring a large pan of lightly salted water to a boil and cook the pasta until it is *al dente*.

2 Meanwhile, heat the oil in a frying pan. Add the onion, garlic and red peppers, and cook over medium heat, stirring frequently, for 5 minutes, until the onion is softened.

3 Stir in the corn kernels and heat through gently, stirring occasionally, for about 5 minutes. Season with salt and pepper to taste.

4 Heat the U-shaped sausage in a pan of simmering water, following the instructions on the package. Do not let the water boil, as this will cause the skin to split. Alternatively, heat the sausage in the microwave, following the instructions on the package.

5 Drain the sausage if necessary, remove the outer covering and slice the meat thinly. Stir the slices into the onion and pepper mixture.

6 Drain the pasta and return it to the clean pan. Add the sauce and chopped basil. Toss well. Serve in a warmed bowl, garnished with the basil sprigs.

Fusilli Lunghi with Sausage & Tomato Sauce

A warming dinner dish, perfect for cold winter nights. Save time by using smoked sausages that only need to be reheated. They are sold, singly, in packages in the refrigerated sections of supermarkets.

Serves 4

1 tablespoon olive oil
1 medium onion, finely chopped
1 red bell pepper, seeded and diced
1 green bell pepper, seeded
  and diced
2 14-ounce cans
  chopped tomatoes
2 tablespoons tomato paste
2 teaspoons mild paprika
4 cups fusilli lunghi
1 reduced-fat U-shaped smoked
  pork sausage
3 tablespoons chopped
  fresh parsley
salt and freshly ground
  black pepper

1 Heat the oil in a medium saucepan. Add the onion and sauté over medium heat, stirring occasionally, for 5 minutes, until it is beginning to color.

2 Stir in the peppers, tomatoes, tomato paste and paprika. Bring to a boil, lower the heat and simmer, uncovered, for 15–20 minutes, until the sauce has reduced and thickened.

3 Meanwhile, bring a large pan of water to a boil, add the pasta and cook until it is *al dente*.

4 Heat the U-shaped sausage in a pan of simmering water, following the instructions on the package. Do not let the water boil, as this will cause the skin to split. Alternatively, heat the sausage in the microwave, following the instructions on the package.

5 Drain the pasta and divide it among four warmed bowls. Drain the sausage, if necessary, remove the outer covering and slice the meat thinly. Add the slices to the sauce, with the parsley, season with salt and pepper to taste and mix well. Top each portion of pasta with sauce and serve immediately.

Tagliatelle with Milanese Sauce

Mushrooms and lean ham in a rich tomato sauce make a tasty topping for tagliatelle.

Serves 4

1 onion, finely chopped
1 celery stalk, finely chopped
1 red bell pepper, seeded
   and diced
1–2 garlic cloves, crushed
²⁄₃ cup vegetable stock
14-ounce can chopped tomatoes
1 tablespoon tomato paste
2 teaspoons sugar
1 teaspoon mixed dried herbs
12 ounces dried tagliatelle,
   preferably mixed colors
1¹⁄₂ cups button
   mushrooms, sliced
¹⁄₄ cup white wine
¹⁄₄ cup lean cooked ham, diced
salt and freshly ground
   black pepper
1 tablespoon chopped fresh
   parsley, to garnish

1 Put the chopped onion, celery, pepper and garlic in a nonstick pan. Add the stock, bring to a boil and cook over medium heat for 5 minutes.

2 Stir in the tomatoes, tomato paste, sugar and dried herbs. Season to taste with salt and pepper. Bring to a boil, then lower the heat and simmer, stirring occasionally, for 30 minutes, until thick.

3 Bring a large pan of lightly salted water to a boil and cook the pasta until it is *al dente*.

4 Meanwhile, put the mushrooms into a heavy pan with the white wine, cover and cook over medium heat for 3–4 minutes, until the mushrooms are tender and all the wine has been absorbed.

5 Stir the mushrooms into the tomato sauce, then add the diced ham.

6 Drain the pasta well and put it in a warmed serving dish. Spoon on the sauce, garnish with the chopped parsley and serve immediately.

Homemade Tortellini

When you make your own tortellini, you are in control of the fat content.

Serves 4–6

4 ounces lean smoked ham
4 ounces skinless, boneless
   chicken breast
3³⁄₄ cups vegetable stock
bunch of cilantro
2 tablespoons grated Parmesan
   cheese, plus extra for serving
1 egg, beaten, plus egg white
   for brushing
1 batch Basic Pasta Dough
all-purpose flour, for dusting
salt and freshly ground
   black pepper

1 Cut the ham and chicken into large chunks and put them into a saucepan with ²⁄₃ cup of the stock. Strip the leaves from the cilantro. Set some aside for the garnish and chop the rest. Add the stalks to the pan. Bring to a boil, cover and simmer for 20 minutes, until the chicken is tender. Set aside to cool slightly.

2 Drain the ham and chicken, reserving the stock, and chop finely. Put the mixture into a bowl and add the Parmesan, beaten egg and chopped cilantro. Season to taste.

3 Roll the pasta into thin sheets, then cut it into 1¹⁄₂-inch squares. Put ¹⁄₂ teaspoon of filling on each. Brush the edges with egg white and fold each square into a triangle. Press out any air and seal firmly.

4 To make the tortellini, curl each triangle around the tip of a forefinger and press two ends together firmly. Lay the tortellini on a lightly floured dish towel to dry out a little for 30 minutes before cooking.

5 Strain the reserved stock into a large pan and add the remainder. Bring to a boil. Lower the heat slightly and add the tortellini. Cook for 5 minutes. Then turn off the heat, cover the pan and let stand for 20–30 minutes. Serve in warmed soup plates with some of the stock. Garnish with the reserved cilantro leaves. Pass grated Parmesan separately.

Pipe Rigate with Peas & Ham

Prettily flecked with pink
and green, this is a lovely
dish for an informal spring
or summer dinner party.

Serves 4
3 cups dried pipe rigate or other
    pasta shapes
1 tablespoon butter
1 tablespoon olive oil
1 1/4–1 1/2 cups frozen
    peas, thawed
1 garlic clove, crushed
2/3 cup chicken stock

2 tablespoons chopped fresh
    flat-leaf parsley
3/4 cup low-fat crème fraîche
4 ounces prosciutto
    crudo, shredded
salt and freshly ground
    black pepper
chopped fresh herbs, such as
    flat-leaf parsley, basil and
    marjoram, to garnish

1 Bring a large pan of lightly salted water to a boil and cook
the pasta until it is *al dente*.

2 Meanwhile, melt half the butter with the olive oil in a
separate pan. Add the peas, garlic and stock. Sprinkle in the
chopped parsley and season with salt and pepper to taste.
Cook over medium heat, stirring frequently, for 5–8 minutes
or until most of the liquid has been absorbed.

3 Add about half the crème fraîche, increase the heat to high
and let the cream bubble, stirring constantly, until it thickens and
coats all the peas. Remove from heat, stir in the prosciutto and
taste for seasoning.

4 Put the cooked pasta in a colander and drain it well.
Immediately add the remaining butter to the pasta pan. When
it has melted, add the remaining crème fraîche and heat until it
is just bubbling.

5 Add the pasta and toss over medium heat until it is evenly
coated. Pour in the pea and ham sauce, toss lightly and heat
through. Spoon into warmed bowls and serve immediately,
sprinkled with fresh herbs.

Ham & Spinach Cannelloni

Keep dried cannelloni tubes
on hand, and tasty dishes
like this one will be easy
to make.

Serves 4
2 tablespoons low-fat spread
1/2 onion, very finely chopped
1 1/2 cups frozen chopped spinach,
    thawed and drained
3 ounces cooked ham, minced or
    very finely diced
1/2 cup fresh white
    bread crumbs
1/2 cup ricotta cheese

1 cup freshly grated reduced-fat
    Parmesan cheese
16 dried no-need-to-precook
    cannelloni tubes
salt and freshly ground
    black pepper

For the white sauce
1/4 cup low-fat spread
1/4 cup all-purpose flour
3 3/4 cups skimmed milk
nutmeg

1 Melt the low-fat spread in a frying pan. Add the onion and
sauté over medium heat, stirring occasionally, for 5 minutes, until
softened but not browned.

2 Add the spinach and cook for 3 minutes, then put the
mixture in a strainer set over a bowl and press the spinach
with the back of a wooden spoon to remove as much liquid
as possible. Discard the liquid.

3 Put the spinach mixture into a separate bowl and stir in the
ham, bread crumbs, ricotta and one-third of the grated
Parmesan. Season with salt and pepper to taste. Preheat the
oven to 375°F.

4 Make the white sauce. Melt the low-fat spread in a saucepan,
add the flour and cook, stirring constantly, for 1–2 minutes.
Gradually add the milk, stirring until the sauce boils and
thickens. Grate in fresh nutmeg to taste, then season with salt
and pepper. Whisk well. Remove the pan from heat.

5 Spoon a little of the white sauce into an ovenproof dish large
enough to hold the cannelloni tubes in a single layer. Fill the
cannelloni tubes with the ham and spinach mixture, and place
them in the dish. Pour on the remaining white sauce, then
sprinkle with the remaining Parmesan.

6 Bake for 35–40 minutes or until the pasta feels tender when
pierced with a skewer. Remove from the oven and let stand for
10 minutes before serving.

Variations
• Use 1 1/4 pounds fresh spinach instead of frozen. Discard any
stems and wash the leaves well in cold water. Transfer to a
saucepan with just the water clinging to the leaves. Cook over
medium heat for 2–3 minutes, until wilted. Turn into a colander
and press out as much liquid as possible. Chop finely and add
to the onions.
• You can also use fresh Swiss chard, which has a similar flavor
and can be prepared in exactly the same way.

Macaroni with Ham & Shrimp

This dinner dish tastes
truly delicious.

Serves 4
3 cups short-cut macaroni
2 tablespoons olive oil
6 ounces smoked
   ham, diced
12 jumbo shrimp, peeled
   and deveined
1 garlic clove, chopped
2/3 cup red wine
1/2 small head of
   radicchio, shredded
2 egg yolks, beaten
2 tablespoons chopped fresh
   flat-leaf parsley
2/3 cup low-fat crème fraîche
salt and freshly ground
   black pepper
shredded fresh basil, to garnish

1 Bring a large pan of salted water to a boil and cook the pasta until it is *al dente*.

2 Meanwhile, heat the oil in a frying pan and cook the ham, shrimp and garlic for about 5 minutes, stirring occasionally until the shrimp have turned pink. Remove the shrimp with a slotted spoon.

3 Add the wine and radicchio to the ham mixture, bring to a boil and boil rapidly until the juices are reduced by half.

4 Stir in the egg yolks, parsley and crème fraîche, and simmer until the sauce thickens slightly. Return the shrimp to the sauce and season to taste.

5 Drain the pasta and return it to the clean pan. Add the sauce and toss to coat. Serve, garnished with shredded fresh basil.

Cook's Tip
Flat-leaf parsley is a pretty herb with more flavor than the curly variety. If you buy a large bunch, finely chop the leftover parsley and freeze it in a small plastic bag. It will then be ready to sprinkle on bubbling soups or casseroles as a garnish.

Pasta with Spinach, Bacon & Mushrooms

Spinach and bacon are
often teamed. Mushrooms
complete the trio in
this recipe.

Serves 4
6 strips bacon,
   cut in small pieces
1 shallot, finely chopped
3 cups small mushrooms,
   quartered
1 pound fresh spinach leaves,
   coarse stems removed
1/4 teaspoon freshly
   grated nutmeg
3 cups dried conchiglie
salt and freshly ground
   black pepper
freshly grated Parmesan cheese,
   to serve (optional)

1 Heat the bacon gently in a frying pan until the fat runs, then raise the heat and cook the bacon until it is crisp. Drain it on paper towels, then put it in a bowl.

2 Add the shallot to the bacon fat in the pan and cook for about 5 minutes, until softened.

3 Add the mushrooms and cook until lightly browned, stirring frequently. With a slotted spoon, add the shallot and mushrooms to the bacon.

4 Pour off most of the bacon fat from the pan, add the spinach and cook over medium heat until wilted, stirring constantly. Sprinkle with the nutmeg, then cook over high heat until the excess liquid from the spinach has evaporated.

5 Transfer the spinach to a board and chop it coarsely. Return it to the pan. Add the bacon mixture and stir well. Season with salt and pepper and keep warm.

6 Bring a large pan of lightly salted water to a boil and cook the pasta until it is *al dente*. Drain it well and return it to the clean pan. Add the spinach mixture and toss well. Serve in warmed bowls, sprinkled with Parmesan, if using.

Ham-filled Paprika Ravioli

Use a ravioli tray to shape these tasty dinner treats.

Serves 4
8 ounces cooked smoked ham
¼ cup mango chutney
1 batch of Basic Pasta Dough,
    with 1 teaspoon ground
    paprika added
egg white, beaten
all-purpose flour, for dusting
1–2 garlic cloves, crushed
1 celery stalk, sliced
2–3 sun-dried tomatoes
1 fresh red chile, seeded
    and chopped
⅔ cup red wine
14-ounce can chopped tomatoes
1 teaspoon chopped fresh thyme,
    plus extra to garnish
2 teaspoons sugar
salt and freshly ground
    black pepper

1 Remove all traces of fat from the ham, place it with the mango chutney in a food processor or blender and grind the mixture finely.

2 Roll the pasta into very thin sheets and lay one piece over a ravioli tray, fitting it carefully into the depressions. Put a teaspoonful of the ham filling into each of the depressions. Brush around the edges of each ravioli with egg white. Cover with another sheet of pasta and press the edges well together to seal.

3 Using a rolling pin, roll over the top of the dough to cut and seal each pocket. Transfer the ravioli to a floured dish towel and let rest for 1 hour before cooking.

4 Put the garlic, celery, sun-dried tomatoes, chile, wine, canned tomatoes and thyme into a pan. Bring to a boil, lower the heat, cover and simmer for 15–20 minutes. Season with salt, pepper and sugar.

5 Bring a large pan of lightly salted water to a boil and cook the ravioli, in batches if necessary, for 4–5 minutes. Drain thoroughly. Spoon a little of the sauce onto each of four warmed serving plates and arrange the ravioli on top. Sprinkle with fresh thyme and serve immediately.

Low-fat Cannelloni

A few simple changes make this version of cannelloni the healthier choice.

Serves 4
2 garlic cloves, crushed
2 14-ounce cans
    chopped tomatoes
2 teaspoons light brown sugar
1 tablespoon shredded fresh basil
1 tablespoon chopped
    fresh marjoram
12–16 dried cannelloni tubes
2 ounces low-fat mozzarella
    cheese, diced
¼ cup grated aged
    Cheddar cheese
½ cup fresh white bread crumbs
salt and freshly ground
    black pepper
fresh flat-leaf parsley, to garnish

For the filling
1 pound frozen chopped spinach
large pinch of freshly
    grated nutmeg
4 ounces cooked lean ham, very
    finely chopped
scant 1 cup low-fat
    cottage cheese

1 Put the garlic, canned tomatoes, sugar and herbs into a pan, bring to a boil and cook, uncovered, for 30 minutes, stirring occasionally, until fairly thick.

2 Make the filling. Put the spinach into a pan, cover and cook slowly until thawed. Break up with a fork, then increase the heat to evaporate any water. Season with salt, pepper and nutmeg. Spoon the spinach into a bowl, let it cool slightly, then add the chopped ham and cottage cheese.

3 Preheat the oven to 350°F. Pipe or spoon the filling into each tube of uncooked cannelloni.

4 Spoon half the tomato sauce into the bottom of an ovenproof dish. Arrange the cannelloni in a single layer on top. Sprinkle on the mozzarella and cover with the rest of the sauce.

5 Sprinkle on the Cheddar cheese and bread crumbs. Bake for 30–40 minutes, browning the top under a hot broiler if necessary. Garnish with the parsley and serve.

Pasta with Deviled Kidneys

The spicy, savory flavor of the kidneys goes particularly well with tender tagliatelle.

Serves 4
8–10 lamb's kidneys
1 tablespoon sunflower oil

1 tablespoon butter
2 teaspoons paprika
1–2 teaspoons mild
    whole-grain mustard
12 ounces fresh tagliatelle
salt
chopped fresh parsley, to garnish

1 Bring a large pan of lightly salted water to a boil. Cut the kidneys in half and neatly cut out the white cores with scissors.

2 Heat the oil and butter together in a frying pan. Add the kidneys and cook, turning frequently, for about 2 minutes.

3 In a cup, mix the paprika and mustard with a little salt. Stir the mixture into the pan and continue to cook the kidneys, basting them frequently, for 3–4 minutes.

4 Meanwhile, bring a large pan of lightly salted water to a boil and cook the pasta until *al dente*, then drain thoroughly and divide among warmed bowls. Top with the kidneys, garnish with the parsley and serve.

Pasta with Deviled Liver

Cook as for Pasta with Deviled Kidneys, but use 1 pound lamb's liver.
1 Trim the liver, removing any skin, and slice it into strips. Toss these in flour, seasoned with plenty of salt and pepper.
2 Use twice as much oil and butter as for the kidneys. Fry the floured liver strips, then stir in the paprika and mustard. Add a generous dash of Tabasco sauce, if desired. Cook for 3–4 minutes, basting the liver frequently.
3 Serve with the fresh tagliatelle, garnished with chopped parsley.

Spaghetti with Meatballs

Meatballs are fun to make and delicious to eat. This is real hands-on cooking!

Serves 4
12 ounces dried spaghetti
4 fresh rosemary sprigs, to garnish
freshly grated Parmesan
    cheese, to serve (optional)

For the meatballs
1 onion, chopped
1 garlic clove, chopped

12 ounces ground lamb
1 egg yolk
1 tablespoon mixed dried herbs
salt and freshly ground
    black pepper
1 tablespoon olive oil

For the sauce
1 1/4 cups passata
2 tablespoons chopped fresh basil
1 garlic clove, chopped

1 Start by making the meatballs. Put the onion, garlic, ground lamb, egg yolk and mixed herbs in a bowl and season to taste with salt and pepper. Combine thoroughly, using a spoon at first, then your hands.

2 Divide the mixture into 20 equal-size pieces and mold into balls. Place on a baking sheet, cover with plastic wrap and chill for about 30 minutes.

3 Heat the oil in a large, heavy frying pan. Add the meatballs and fry over medium heat, turning occasionally, for about 10 minutes, until browned all over.

4 Add all the sauce ingredients and bring to a boil. Cover, lower the heat and simmer for about 20 minutes, until the meatballs are tender.

5 Bring a large pan of lightly salted water to a boil and cook the pasta until it is *al dente*.

6 Drain the pasta thoroughly and divide it among four warmed serving plates. Spoon over the meatballs and some of the sauce. Garnish each portion with a fresh rosemary sprig and serve immediately with Parmesan, if using.

Spirali with Rich Meat Sauce

The sauce definitely improves if kept overnight in the refrigerator. This gives the flavors enough time to mature. There isn't any wine in this meat sauce, but the bacon and red currant jelly give it a fine flavor.

Serves 4

1 tablespoon vegetable oil
1 pound lean ground beef
4 ounces lean bacon, chopped
1 onion, chopped
2 celery stalks, chopped
2/3 cup chicken stock
3 tablespoons tomato paste
1 garlic clove, chopped
3 tablespoons chopped mixed
   fresh herbs
1 tablespoon red currant jelly
3 cups dried spirali
salt and freshly ground
   black pepper
chopped fresh oregano, to garnish

1 Heat the oil in a large saucepan. Add the beef and bacon, and cook over medium heat, stirring occasionally, for about 10 minutes, until browned.

2 Add the onion and celery, and cook for 5 minutes, stirring occasionally, then put the contents of the pan in a metal colander and drain off the excess fat. Return the meat mixture to the pan.

3 Stir in the stock, tomato paste, garlic, herbs and red currant jelly. Season well, bring to a boil, then lower the heat, cover and simmer for at least 30 minutes, stirring occasionally.

4 Bring a large pan of lightly salted water to a boil and cook the pasta until it is *al dente*. Drain thoroughly and turn it into a large serving bowl. Pour on the sauce and toss to coat. Serve immediately, garnished with chopped fresh oregano.

> **Variation**
> *You can use sweet mint jelly or chutney instead of the red currant jelly.*

Mock Bolognese

This doesn't pretend to be anything like the real thing, but Worcestershire sauce, chili and spicy pork sausages ensure that it is full of flavor and makes a very good family meal.

Serves 4

1 tablespoon vegetable oil
1 onion, chopped
8 ounces ground beef
1 teaspoon mild chili powder
1 tablespoon Worcestershire sauce
2 tablespoons all-purpose flour
2/3 cup beef stock
4 reduced-fat spicy pork
   sausages, sliced
7-ounce can chopped tomatoes
1/3 cup baby corn, halved
   lengthwise
1 tablespoon chopped fresh basil
12 ounces dried spaghetti
salt and freshly ground
   black pepper
fresh basil sprigs, to garnish

1 Heat the oil in a large saucepan. Add the onion and ground beef, and fry over medium heat for 5 minutes, stirring to break up any lumps.

2 Add the chili powder and cook, stirring constantly, for another 3 minutes.

3 Stir in the Worcestershire sauce and flour. Cook for 1 minute, stirring constantly, then gradually pour in the stock, stirring constantly. Stir in the sliced sausages, tomatoes, baby corn and chopped basil. Season with salt and pepper to taste, and bring to a boil. Lower the heat and simmer for 30 minutes.

4 Bring a large pan of lightly salted water to a boil and cook the pasta until it is *al dente*.

5 Drain, place on four individual plates and top with the meat sauce. Garnish with the basil sprigs.

> **Cook's Tip**
> *Make the mock Bolognese sauce and freeze in conveniently sized portions for up to two months.*

Ground Beef & Pipe Rigate

Cheer up a chilly evening with this hearty, warming and colorful dish.

Serves 6
1 pound extra lean ground beef
1 onion, finely chopped
2–3 garlic cloves, crushed
1–2 fresh red chiles, seeded and finely chopped
14-ounce can chopped tomatoes
3 tablespoons tomato paste
1 teaspoon mixed dried herbs
1¾ cups water
4 cups dried pipe rigate
14-ounce can red kidney beans, drained
salt and freshly ground black pepper

1 Dry-fry the ground beef in a heavy nonstick saucepan over medium heat, breaking up any lumps with a wooden spoon, until browned all over. Drain off any fat that has run from the meat.

2 Add the onion, garlic and chiles, and lower the heat. Cover and cook gently, stirring occasionally, for 5 minutes.

3 Stir in the tomatoes, tomato paste, herbs and measured water. Bring to a boil, then lower the heat and simmer for 1½ hours. Season to taste with salt and pepper and set aside to cool slightly.

4 Bring a large pan of lightly salted water to a boil and cook the pasta until it is *al dente*.

5 Meanwhile, stir the kidney beans into the meat sauce and heat through, stirring occasionally, for about 10 minutes.

6 Drain the pasta and arrange it on warmed plates. Pile the sauce in the center and serve immediately.

> **Cook's Tip**
> *If you make the sauce the day before, it will be even more flavorful and you can also skim off any residual fat.*

Low-fat Spaghetti Bolognese

Mushrooms are a gift to the health-conscious cook, as long as they are cooked in wine and not fat.

Serves 8
1 medium onion, chopped
2–3 garlic cloves, crushed
1¼ cups defatted beef or chicken stock
1 pound ground turkey or extra lean beef
2 14-ounce cans chopped tomatoes
1 teaspoon dried basil
1 teaspoon dried oregano
¼ cup tomato paste
6 cups button mushrooms, sliced
⅔ cup red wine
1 pound dried spaghetti
salt and freshly ground black pepper

1 Put the chopped onion and crushed garlic in a pan and pour in half of the stock. Bring to a boil and cook for 5 minutes, until the onion is tender and very little stock remains.

2 Add the turkey or beef and cook over medium heat for 5 minutes, breaking up any lumps with a fork.

3 Stir in the chopped tomatoes, herbs, remaining beef or chicken stock and tomato paste, and bring to a boil. Lower the heat, cover and simmer for about 1 hour.

4 Meanwhile, put the button mushrooms into a nonstick frying pan with the wine, bring to a boil and cook for 5 minutes or until the wine has been absorbed. Add the cooked mushrooms to the meat sauce and season to taste with salt and freshly ground black pepper. Keep the sauce hot while you cook the pasta.

5 Bring a large pan of lightly salted water to a boil and cook the spaghetti until it is *al dente*. Drain thoroughly. Transfer to individual warmed plates, top with the meat sauce and serve.

Meatballs with Cream Sauce

Three types of meat make these meatballs extra special.

Serves 6
2 tablespoons low-fat spread
½ onion, finely chopped
8 ounces lean ground beef
4 ounces lean ground veal
8 ounces lean ground pork
1 egg
4 ounces cooked
   mashed potatoes
2 tablespoons chopped fresh dill
1 garlic clove, finely chopped

½ teaspoon ground allspice
¼ teaspoon grated nutmeg
¾ cup fresh white bread crumbs,
   soaked in ¾ cup skimmed milk
about ⅓ cup all-purpose flour
2 tablespoons olive oil
1 pound dried tagliatelli
⅔ cup reduced-fat light cream
salt and freshly ground
   black pepper
fresh dill sprigs, to garnish

1 Melt half the low-fat spread in a pan and cook the onion over low heat, until softened. Transfer the onion to a bowl, using a slotted spoon.

2 Add the ground meats, egg, mashed potatoes, dill, garlic, spices and seasoning to the bowl. Add the soaked bread crumbs and mix well.

3 Shape the mixture into balls about 1 inch in diameter. Coat them lightly in flour. Heat the oil in a large frying pan and cook the meatballs for 8–10 minutes, until brown on all sides, shaking the pan occasionally.

4 Meanwhile, bring a large pan of lightly salted water to a boil and cook the pasta until it is *al dente*.

5 Using a slotted spoon, transfer the meatballs to a dish and keep them hot. Stir 1 tablespoon flour into the fat in the frying pan. Whisk in the cream, then simmer for 3–4 minutes.

6 Drain the pasta and toss it with the remaining low-fat spread. Divide among six warmed plates, and top each with a portion of meatballs and sauce. Garnish with dill and serve.

Pasta Timbales

An alternative way to serve pasta for a special occasion. Mixed with ground beef and tomato, and baked in a lettuce parcel, it makes an impressive dish.

Serves 4
8 Romaine lettuce leaves
fresh basil sprigs, to garnish

For the filling
1 tablespoon vegetable oil
6 ounces ground beef

1 tablespoon tomato paste
1 garlic clove, crushed
1 cup dried short-cut macaroni
salt and freshly ground
   black pepper

For the sauce
2 tablespoons low-fat spread
¼ cup all-purpose flour
1 cup low-fat crème fraîche
2 tablespoons chopped fresh basil

1 Preheat the oven to 350°F. Make the filling. Heat the oil in a large pan and fry the beef for 7 minutes. Add the tomato paste and garlic, and cook for 5 minutes.

2 Meanwhile, bring a large pan of lightly salted water to a boil and cook the macaroni until it is *al dente*. Drain the macaroni and stir it into the meat sauce.

3 Line four ⅔-cup ramekins with the lettuce leaves, overlapping the sides. Season the meat mixture and spoon it into the lettuce-lined ramekins. Fold the lettuce leaves over the filling. Stand the ramekins in a roasting pan and pour in boiling water to come halfway up the sides. Cover the pan with aluminum foil and bake for 20 minutes.

4 While the timbales are cooking, make the sauce. Melt the low-fat spread in a pan. Add the flour and cook, stirring constantly, for 1 minute. Gradually add the crème fraîche, stirring until the sauce boils and thickens. Stir in the basil, with salt and pepper to taste.

5 Turn out the timbales onto warmed plates and pour the sauce around them. Garnish with the basil sprigs and serve.

Special Chow Mein

This famous dish can be as simple or as elaborate as you like. This is a particularly luxurious version.

Serves 6

1 pound dried egg noodles
4 teaspoons vegetable oil
2 garlic cloves, sliced
1 teaspoon chopped fresh
   ginger root
2 fresh red chiles, chopped
2 lap cheong sausages, rinsed
   and sliced

1 skinless, boneless chicken
   breast, thinly sliced
16 tiger shrimp, peeled, tails left
   intact, and deveined
4 ounces green beans
4 cups bean sprouts
1 cup garlic chives
2 tablespoons soy sauce
1 tablespoon oyster sauce
salt and freshly ground
   black pepper
shredded scallions and cilantro
   leaves, to garnish

1 Bring a large pan of lightly salted water to a boil and cook the noodles until they are just tender, checking the package for information on timing. Drain, rinse under cold water and drain thoroughly again.

2 Preheat a wok and swirl in half the oil. When it is hot, add the garlic, ginger and chiles, and stir-fry over medium heat for 1 minute.

3 Add the lap cheong slices, chicken, shrimp and beans. Stir-fry for about 2 minutes or until the chicken is cooked and the shrimp have changed color. Transfer the mixture to a bowl and set aside.

4 Heat the rest of the oil in the wok, add the bean sprouts and garlic chives, and stir-fry for 1–2 minutes. Add the noodles, and toss and stir to mix. Stir in the soy sauce and oyster sauce, and season to taste with salt and pepper.

5 Return the shrimp mixture to the wok and toss over the heat until well mixed and heated through. Transfer the noodle mixture to warmed bowls, garnish with scallions and cilantro leaves, and serve immediately.

Singapore Rice Vermicelli

A lighter rice vermicelli noodle dish, this time made with ham.

Serves 4

2 teaspoons vegetable oil
1 egg, lightly beaten
2 garlic cloves, finely chopped
1 large fresh red or green chile,
   seeded and finely chopped
1 tablespoon medium
   curry powder
1 red bell pepper, seeded and
   thinly sliced

1 green bell pepper, seeded and
   thinly sliced
1 carrot, cut into matchsticks
¼ teaspoon salt
¼ cup vegetable stock
8 ounces diced rice vermicelli,
   soaked in warm water until soft
4 ounces cooked peeled shrimp,
   thawed if frozen
3 ounces lean cooked ham, cut
   into ½-inch cubes
1 tablespoon light soy sauce

1 Preheat a wok and swirl in 1 teaspoon of the oil. When it is hot, add the egg and scramble until just set. Remove with a slotted spoon and set aside.

2 Heat the remaining oil in the clean wok, add the garlic and chile, and stir-fry for a few seconds. Add the curry powder. Cook for 1 minute, stirring constantly, then stir in the peppers, carrot sticks, salt and stock.

3 Drain the rice vermicelli thoroughly. Heat the contents of the wok until the stock boils. Add the shrimp, ham, scrambled egg, rice vermicelli and soy sauce. Mix thoroughly. Cook, stirring constantly, until all the liquid has been absorbed and the mixture is hot. Serve immediately.

> **Cook's Tip**
> *Curry powder varies in flavor, content and degree of heat from brand to brand. Most contain varying proportions of ground cardamom, chile, cloves, coriander, cumin, ginger, nutmeg, pepper, tamarind and turmeric. They may also contain ajowan, caraway, fennel and mustard seeds.*

Udon Pot

Fast food Japanese-style—it's a simple formula, but a winning one. First-class ingredients simmered in a good stock make a great dish.

Serves 4

1 large carrot, cut into bite-size chunks
12 ounces dried udon noodles
8 ounces skinless, boneless chicken breasts, cut into bite-size pieces
8 jumbo shrimp, peeled and deveined
4–6 Chinese cabbage leaves, cut into short strips
8 fresh shiitake mushrooms, stems removed
1/2 cup snow peas, trimmed
6 cups defatted homemade chicken stock or instant bonito stock
2 tablespoons mirin
soy sauce, to taste
finely chopped scallions, grated fresh ginger root, lemon wedges and extra soy sauce, to serve

1 Bring a large pan of lightly salted water to a boil and add the carrot chunks. Blanch for 1 minute, then lift out with a slotted spoon and set aside.

2 Add the noodles to the boiling water and cook until just tender, checking the package for information on timing. Drain, rinse under cold water and drain again.

3 Spoon the carrot chunks and noodles into a large shallow pan or wok and arrange the chicken, shrimp, Chinese cabbage leaves, mushrooms and snow peas on top.

4 Bring the stock to a boil in a separate saucepan. Add the mirin and soy sauce to taste. Pour the stock onto the noodle mixture and bring to a boil. Lower the heat, cover, then simmer over medium heat for 5–6 minutes, until all the ingredients are cooked and tender.

5 Spoon the noodle mixture into a warmed dish and serve immediately with side dishes of chopped scallions, grated ginger, lemon wedges and a little soy sauce.

Egg Fried Noodles

Yellow bean sauce gives these seafood noodles a savory flavor.

Serves 4–6

12 ounces medium-thick dried egg noodles
2 tablespoons vegetable oil
4 scallions, cut into 1/2-inch rounds
juice of 1 lime
1 tablespoon soy sauce
2 garlic cloves, finely chopped
6 ounces skinless, boneless chicken breast, sliced
6 ounces shrimp, peeled and deveined
6 ounces squid, cleaned and cut into rings
1 tablespoon yellow bean sauce
1 tablespoon Thai fish sauce
1 tablespoon light brown sugar
1 egg
cilantro leaves, to garnish

1 Bring a large pan of lightly salted water to a boil and cook the noodles until they are just tender, checking the package for information on timing. Drain well.

2 Preheat a wok and swirl in half the oil. When it is hot, stir-fry the scallions over medium heat for 2 minutes, then add the drained noodles, with the lime juice and soy sauce. Stir-fry for another 2–3 minutes. Transfer the mixture to a bowl and keep it hot.

3 Heat the remaining oil in the wok. Add the garlic, chicken, shrimp and squid. Stir-fry over high heat until the chicken and seafood are cooked.

4 Stir in the yellow bean sauce, fish sauce and sugar, then break the egg into the mixture, stirring gently until it sets in threads.

5 Add the noodles, toss lightly to mix, and heat through. Transfer to warmed bowls, garnish with cilantro leaves and serve immediately.

Sweet-and-Sour Chicken Noodles

This all-in-one dish is the busy cook's answer to that perennial question of what to cook for dinner when time is short and everyone is hungry.

Serves 4

10 ounces dried egg noodles
1 tablespoon vegetable oil
3 scallions, chopped
1 garlic clove, crushed
1-inch piece of fresh ginger
   root, grated
1 teaspoon hot paprika
1 teaspoon ground coriander
3 skinless, boneless chicken
   breasts, sliced
1 cup sugar snap peas, trimmed
⅔ cup baby corn, halved
4 cups fresh bean sprouts, rinsed
1 tablespoon cornstarch
3 tablespoons soy sauce
3 tablespoons lemon juice
1 tablespoon sugar
3 tablespoons chopped cilantro,
   to garnish

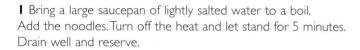

1 Bring a large saucepan of lightly salted water to a boil. Add the noodles. Turn off the heat and let stand for 5 minutes. Drain well and reserve.

2 Preheat a wok. Add the oil. When it is hot, stir-fry the scallions until softened. Stir in the garlic, ginger, paprika, ground coriander and chicken slices. Stir-fry for 3–4 minutes.

3 Add the sugar snap peas, corn and bean sprouts. Toss to mix, then cover and steam for 2–3 minutes, until the sugar snap peas are crisp-tender. Add the noodles and toss over the heat.

4 Stir the cornstarch, soy sauce, lemon juice and sugar together in a small bowl. Add to the chicken mixture and simmer briefly to thicken. Serve immediately in heated bowls, garnished with chopped cilantro.

Cook's Tip
Light soy sauce has a stronger flavor than the sweeter dark variety, but the latter adds more color to a dish.

Chicken Chow Mein

Dried egg noodles need very little cooking and are perfect for quick and tasty stir-fried dishes such as this old family favorite.

Serves 4

8 ounces skinless, boneless
   chicken breasts
3 tablespoons soy sauce
1 tablespoon rice wine or
   dry sherry
a few drops of dark sesame oil
12 ounces dried egg noodles
1 tablespoon vegetable oil
2 garlic cloves, finely chopped
½ cup snow peas, trimmed
2 cups bean sprouts, rinsed
2 ounces lean ham,
   finely shredded
4 scallions, finely chopped
salt and freshly ground
   black pepper

1 Using a sharp knife, slice the chicken into very fine shreds about 2 inches long. Place in a bowl and add 2 teaspoons of the soy sauce, with the rice wine or sherry and the sesame oil. Mix well, then set aside.

2 Bring a large pan of lightly salted water to a boil and add the noodles. Turn off the heat and let stand for 5 minutes. Drain well and reserve.

3 Preheat a wok and add half the vegetable oil. When it is very hot, add the chicken mixture and stir-fry for 2 minutes, then transfer it to a plate and keep it hot.

4 Wipe the wok clean and heat the remaining oil. Stir in the garlic, snow peas, bean sprouts and shredded ham, and stir-fry for another minute or so. Add the noodles.

5 Toss the noodles over the heat until they are heated through. Add the remaining soy sauce and season with pepper to taste, and salt, if necessary.

6 Return the chicken and any juices to the noodle mixture, add the chopped scallions and toss the mixture once more. Serve immediately in heated bowls.

Stir-fried Turkey with Broccoli & Mushrooms

This is a really easy, tasty dinner dish.

Serves 4

10 ounces dried egg noodles
scant 1 cup broccoli florets
1 teaspoon cornstarch
3 tablespoons oyster sauce
1 tablespoon dark soy sauce
½ cup chicken stock
2 teaspoons lemon juice
2 tablespoons peanut oil
1 pound turkey steaks, cut into
　thin strips
1 small onion, chopped
2 garlic cloves, crushed
2 teaspoons grated fresh
　ginger root
1½ cups fresh shiitake
　mushrooms, sliced
4 ears of baby corn,
　halved lengthwise
2 teaspoons sesame oil
salt and freshly ground
　black pepper
4 scallions

1 Bring a large pan of lightly salted water to a boil and add the noodles. Cover, remove from heat and let stand. Divide the broccoli florets into sprigs and thinly slice the stalks diagonally. Finely chop the white parts of the scallions and thinly shred the green parts.

2 In a bowl, combine the cornstarch, oyster sauce, soy sauce, stock and lemon juice. Set aside.

3 Preheat a wok. Add 1 tablespoon of the peanut oil. When hot, stir-fry the turkey for 2 minutes, until golden and crispy at the edges. Remove the turkey from the wok and keep it hot.

4 Add the remaining peanut oil to the wok and stir-fry the onion, garlic and ginger for 1 minute. Increase the heat, add the broccoli, mushrooms and corn, and stir-fry for 2 minutes.

5 Return the turkey to the wok, then add the sauce with the seasoning. Cook, stirring for 1 minute, until the sauce has thickened. Stir in the sesame oil. Drain the noodles and serve with the stir-fry. Sprinkle the scallions on top.

Duck with Noodles, Pineapple & Ginger

As striking as any still-life, but substantially more satisfying for dinner.

Serves 2–3

4 scallions, chopped
2 boneless duck breasts, skinned
1 tablespoon light soy sauce
6 ounces dried egg noodles
8-ounce can pineapple rings
5 tablespoons water
4 pieces of drained Chinese
　stem ginger in syrup, plus
　3 tablespoons syrup from the jar
2 tablespoons cornstarch mixed to
　a paste with a little water
6 ounces each cooked baby spinach
　and blanched green beans
¼ each red and green bell pepper,
　seeded and cut into thin strips
salt and freshly ground black pepper

1 Select a shallow bowl that fits into your steamer and that will accommodate the duck breasts side by side. Spread out the scallions in the bowl, arrange the duck breasts on top and drizzle on the soy sauce. Cover with nonstick baking parchment. Set the steamer over boiling water and cook the duck breasts for about 1 hour or until tender. Remove the breasts from the steamer and let cool slightly.

2 Cut the breasts into thin slices. Place on a plate, moisten with a little of the cooking juices and keep warm. Strain the remaining juices into a small saucepan and set aside.

3 Bring a large pan of lightly salted water to a boil and cook the noodles until they are just tender.

4 Meanwhile, drain the pineapple, reserving 5 tablespoons of the juice. Add this to the reserved cooking juices, with the measured water. Stir in the ginger syrup, then stir in the cornstarch paste and cook, stirring until thickened. Season.

5 Cut the pineapple and ginger into attractive shapes. Drain the noodles and swirl them into nest shapes on individual plates. Add the spinach and beans, then the duck. Top with the pineapple, ginger and peppers. Pour on the sauce and serve.

Pork & Noodle Stir-fry

This tasty Chinese dish is both very easy to prepare and healthy.

Serves 4
8 ounces dried egg noodles
1 tablespoon vegetable oil
1 onion, chopped
½-inch piece fresh ginger
  root, chopped
2 garlic cloves, crushed

2 tablespoons soy sauce
¼ cup dry white wine
2 teaspoons Chinese
  five-spice powder
1 pound lean ground pork
4 scallions, sliced
¾ cup oyster mushrooms
½ cup drained canned sliced
  bamboo shoots
sesame oil, to serve (optional)

1 Bring a large pan of lightly salted water to a boil and cook the noodles until they are just tender, checking the package for timing. Drain, rinse under cold water and drain well again.

2 Preheat a wok and swirl in the oil. When it is hot, add the onion, ginger, garlic, soy sauce and wine. Cook for 1 minute. Stir in the Chinese five-spice powder.

3 Add the pork and cook for 10 minutes, stirring continuously. Add the scallions, mushrooms and bamboo shoots, and cook for 5 more minutes.

4 Stir in the drained noodles, and toss over the heat until they are heated through and have mixed with the other ingredients. Drizzle on a little sesame oil, if using, and serve immediately.

Indonesian Pork & Noodles

This spicy noodle dish couldn't be easier.

Serves 4
8 ounces broccoli, divided
  into florets
8 ounces egg noodles
1 tablespoon peanut oil
8 ounces boneless loin of pork,
  cut into thin strips
1 carrot, cut into matchsticks

1 onion, finely chopped
2 garlic cloves, crushed
1 teaspoon grated fresh ginger root
½ teaspoon dried shrimp paste
½ teaspoon sambal oelek
4 Chinese cabbage
  leaves, shredded
2 tablespoons light soy sauce,
  plus extra to serve
2 teaspoons sugar
salt

1 Bring a large pan of lightly salted water to a boil and blanch the broccoli for 1 minute. Remove with a slotted spoon.
2 Bring the water back to a boil and cook the noodles until they are just tender, checking the package for information on timing. Drain, rinse under cold water and drain well again.
3 Preheat a wok and swirl in the oil. Add the pork, carrot, onion, garlic, ginger, shrimp paste and sambal oelek, and stir-fry over medium to high heat for 3–4 minutes.
4 Add the broccoli and Chinese cabbage leaves, and stir-fry for 1 minute more.
5 Add the noodles, soy sauce and sugar, and stir-fry for 3–4 minutes, until heated through. Transfer to a warmed serving dish and serve immediately with extra soy sauce.

Lemongrass Pork

Chiles and lemongrass flavor this simple stir-fry, while peanuts add crunch.

Serves 4
1 pound boneless loin of pork
2 lemongrass stalks, trimmed and
  finely chopped
4 scallions, thinly sliced
1 teaspoon salt
12 black peppercorns,
  coarsely crushed
1 tablespoon peanut oil
2 garlic cloves, chopped

2 fresh red chiles, seeded
  and chopped
8 ounces dried rice vermicelli,
  soaked in warm water until soft
1 teaspoon light brown sugar
2 tablespoons fish sauce
¼ cup roasted unsalted
  peanuts, chopped
salt and freshly ground
  black pepper
roughly torn cilantro leaves,
  to garnish

1 Trim any fat from the pork. Cut the meat across into ¼-inch thick slices, then into ¼-inch strips. Put them in a bowl with the lemongrass, scallions, salt and peppercorns. Mix well, cover and let marinate for 30 minutes.

2 Heat a wok and swirl in the oil. When it is hot, stir-fry the pork for 3 minutes. Add the garlic and chiles, and stir-fry for 5–8 more minutes, until the pork no longer looks pink.

3 Meanwhile, bring a large pan of lightly salted water to a boil. Drain the rice vermicelli, add it to the water and cook briefly until just tender. Drain thoroughly and pile onto a warmed serving dish.

4 Add the sugar, fish sauce and peanuts to the pork mixture and toss to mix. Taste and adjust the seasoning, if necessary. Spoon onto the dish, alongside the noodles, garnish with the cilantro leaves and serve.

Variation
Use skinless, boneless chicken breast if you prefer it to pork.

Beef & Broccoli Stir-fry

A quick-to-make dish with Eastern appeal.

Serves 4
2 teaspoons cornstarch
3 tablespoons soy sauce
3 tablespoons port
1 tablespoon sunflower oil
12 ounces lean beef,
    cut into thin strips
1 garlic clove, crushed
1-inch piece of fresh ginger root,
    finely chopped
1 red bell pepper, seeded
    and sliced
1½ cups small broccoli florets
12 ounces rice vermicelli, soaked
    in warm water until soft
fresh parsley sprigs, to garnish

1 Mix the cornstarch, soy sauce and port in a small bowl.

2 Preheat a wok. Add the oil. When hot, stir-fry the beef, garlic and ginger until the beef is browned. Add the red pepper and broccoli, and stir-fry for 4–5 minutes, until just tender.

3 Stir the cornstarch mixture into the wok. Cook, stirring constantly, until the sauce thickens and becomes glossy. Drain the vermicelli, add it to the wok and toss over the heat for 2–3 minutes, until heated through. Serve in warmed bowls, garnished with parsley.

Variations
You could use red wine if you do not have port. Try using other vegetables such as snow peas, sugar snap peas or fresh asparagus instead of the broccoli.

Rice Noodles with Beef & Black Bean Sauce

This is an excellent combination—beef with a chili sauce tossed with silky smooth rice noodles.

Serves 4
1 pound fresh flat rice noodles
2 tablespoons vegetable oil
1 onion, finely sliced
2 garlic cloves, finely chopped
2 slices of fresh ginger root,
    finely chopped
8 ounces mixed bell peppers,
    seeded and cut into strips
12 ounces lean rump steak,
    finely sliced against the grain
3 tablespoons fermented black
    beans, rinsed in warm water,
    drained and chopped
2 tablespoons soy sauce
2 tablespoons oyster sauce
1 tablespoon chili black
    bean sauce
1 tablespoon cornstarch
½ cup stock or water
salt and freshly ground
    black pepper
2 scallions, finely chopped, and
    2 fresh red chiles, seeded and
    finely sliced, to garnish

1 Rinse the noodles under hot water and drain well. Preheat a wok. Add two tablespoons of the oil. When hot, stir-fry the onion, garlic, ginger and mixed pepper strips for 3–5 minutes. Remove with a slotted spoon and keep hot.

2 Add the remaining oil to the wok. When hot, add the sliced beef and fermented black beans, and stir-fry over high heat for 5 minutes or until they are cooked.

3 In a small bowl, mix the soy sauce, oyster sauce and chili black bean sauce with the cornstarch and stock or water until smooth. Add the cornstarch paste to the beef mixture in the wok, then stir in the onion mixture. Cook over medium heat, stirring constantly, for 1 minute.

4 Add the noodles and mix lightly. Toss over medium heat, until the noodles are heated through. Adjust the seasoning if necessary. Serve immediately, garnished with the chopped scallions and chiles.

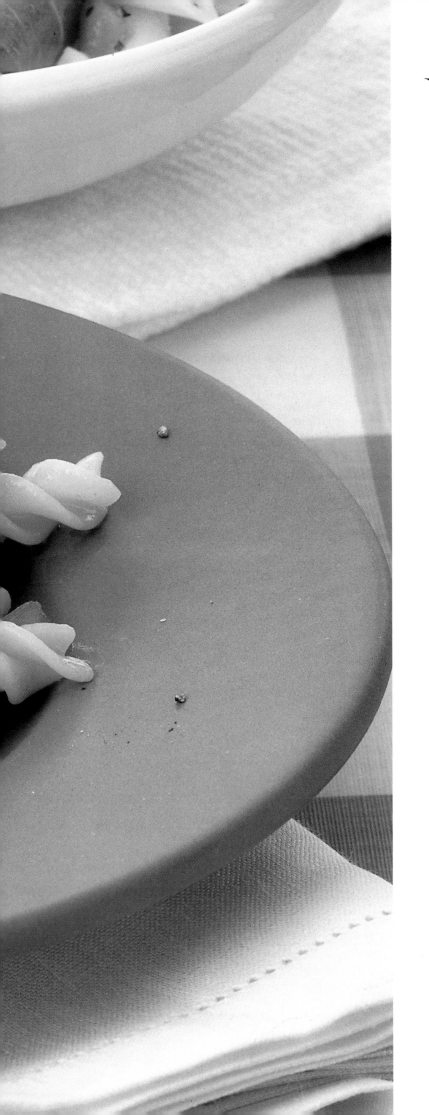

VEGETARIAN PASTA

Eliche with Bell Peppers

This is a dish for high summer when peppers and tomatoes ripen naturally and are plentiful. It is equally good cold as a salad.

Serves 4
3 large bell peppers (red, yellow and orange)
3 cups fresh or dried eliche
1–2 garlic cloves, finely chopped

4 ripe Italian plum tomatoes, peeled, seeded and diced
½ cup pitted black olives, halved or quartered lengthwise
¼ cup extra virgin olive oil
a handful of fresh basil leaves
salt and freshly ground black pepper

1 Preheat the broiler. Cut the peppers in half, remove the cores and seeds, and place them cut-side down in the broiler pan. Broil until the skins have blistered and begun to char.

2 Put the peppers in a bowl, cover with several layers of paper towels and set aside for 10 minutes.

3 Bring a large pan of lightly salted water to a boil and cook the pasta until it is *al dente*.

4 While the pasta is cooking, peel the peppers, slice the flesh thinly and place it in a large bowl.

5 Add the garlic, tomatoes, olives and olive oil to the peppers. Mix lightly, then add salt and pepper to taste.

6 Drain the cooked pasta and put it in the bowl. Add the basil leaves. Toss thoroughly to mix and serve immediately in warmed bowls.

Variation
A few strips of sun-dried tomatoes would give this even more flavor. Choose the type in oil, and use some of the oil in the dressing, if desired.

Capellini with Bell Peppers & Snow Peas

The vegetables in this pretty, summery dish are barely cooked—rather, they are just heated through. As a result, they stay crisp, providing a contrast to the tender pasta.

Serves 4
12 ounces dried capellini
2 teaspoons peanut oil
2 tablespoons cornstarch
2 tablespoons water
2 teaspoons vegetable oil
3 garlic cloves, finely chopped
¾ cup vegetable stock
3 tablespoons dry sherry
1 tablespoon sesame oil

1 tablespoon light soy sauce
1 teaspoon chili sauce
½ teaspoon sugar
½ teaspoon Szechuan peppercorns, crushed
1 red bell pepper, seeded and cut into strips
1 yellow bell pepper, seeded and cut into strips
4 ounces snow peas, trimmed and halved
10 button mushrooms, thinly sliced
3 scallions
pared zest of 1 orange, thinly shredded, to garnish

1 Bring a large pan of lightly salted water to a boil and cook the pasta until it is *al dente*. Drain in a colander, then transfer to a large bowl and stir in the peanut oil.

2 Put the cornstarch in a small bowl and stir in the measured water to make a smooth paste.

3 Preheat a wok or large, heavy frying pan and add the vegetable oil. When it is hot, add the garlic and stir-fry for about 20 seconds. Add the vegetable stock, sherry, sesame oil, soy sauce, chili sauce, sugar and Szechuan peppercorns. Bring to a boil, stirring constantly. Pour in the cornstarch mixture, stirring constantly until slightly thickened.

4 Add the pasta and vegetables to the wok. Toss over the heat for about 2 minutes or until the mixture is hot. Serve immediately, garnished with the orange zest.

Tagliatelle with Tomato & Mushroom Sauce

Using dried mushrooms adds extra concentrated flavor to the sauce.

Serves 4
1/2 cup dried Italian mushrooms (porcini)
3/4 cup hot water
2 pounds tomatoes, peeled, seeded and chopped
1/4 teaspoon dried hot chile flakes

1 large garlic clove, finely chopped
12 ounces dried tagliatelle or fettuccine
1 teaspoon olive oil
salt and freshly ground black pepper
freshly grated Parmesan cheese, to serve

1 Put the dried mushrooms in a bowl and pour in the hot water to cover. Let soak for 20 minutes.

2 Meanwhile, put the tomatoes in a saucepan and add the chile flakes. Bring to a boil, lower the heat and simmer, stirring occasionally, for 30–40 minutes or until thick.

3 When the mushrooms have finished soaking, lift them out and squeeze them over the bowl. Set them aside. Carefully pour the soaking liquid into the tomatoes through a muslin-lined strainer, leaving any sandy grit in the bottom of the bowl. Simmer the tomato sauce for 15 more minutes.

4 Meanwhile, place the garlic and mushrooms in a nonstick frying pan and dry-fry over low heat for 3 minutes, stirring. Add to the tomato sauce and mix well. Season with salt and pepper, and keep hot.

5 Bring a large pan of lightly salted water to a boil and cook the pasta until it is *al dente*. Drain it well and return it to the pan. Toss with the oil. Divide among warmed plates, spoon the sauce on top and serve with Parmesan cheese.

Penne with Broccoli & Chili

Chunky, with just enough "bite" to provide an interesting contrast to the broccoli, penne are perfect in this easy dish.

Serves 4
3 cups dried penne
generous 3 cups small broccoli florets

2 tablespoons vegetable stock
1 garlic clove, crushed
1 small fresh red chile, sliced, or 1/2 teaspoon chili sauce
1/4 cup low-fat plain yogurt
2 tablespoons toasted pine nuts or cashews
salt and freshly ground black pepper

1 Bring a pan of lightly salted water to a boil and add the pasta. When the water returns to a boil, place the broccoli in a steamer basket set on top. Cover and cook for 8–10 minutes, until both the pasta and the broccoli are just tender.

2 When the pasta is almost ready, heat the stock in a separate pan, and add the garlic and chile or chili sauce. Stir over low heat for 2–3 minutes.

3 Drain the pasta and stir it into the flavored stock, with the broccoli and yogurt. Season to taste with salt and pepper, put in a warmed serving bowl and sprinkle with the toasted nuts. Serve immediately.

Variations
• You could substitute green Tabasco sauce for the chile if you like a "kick" of spice but prefer something a little milder.
• For a slightly richer taste, you could use smetana instead of low-fat yogurt.

Farfalle with Red Bell Pepper Sauce

A quick and easy sauce that tastes great with pasta.

Serves 4
4 cups dried farfalle
2 large red bell peppers, seeded and finely diced
1 garlic clove, crushed

3 ripe tomatoes, peeled, seeded and chopped
1/2 cup vegetable stock
1 teaspoon balsamic vinegar
salt and freshly ground black pepper
chopped fresh herbs, to garnish

1 Bring a large pan of lightly salted water to a boil and cook the pasta until it is *al dente*.
2 Meanwhile, make the sauce. Set about 3 tablespoons of the diced red pepper aside for the garnish. Put the rest in a pan with the garlic, tomatoes and stock. Bring to a boil, then lower the heat and simmer, stirring occasionally, until the mixture is thick. Stir in the balsamic vinegar and season to taste.
3 Drain the pasta, put it in a warmed bowl and toss with the red pepper sauce. Garnish with the reserved red pepper and chopped herbs, and serve.

Pasta Napoletana

Classic cooked tomato sauce makes a healthy choice, when served with pasta and not too much Parmesan cheese.

Serves 4

2 pounds fresh ripe red tomatoes
1 medium onion, chopped
1 medium carrot, diced
1 celery stalk, diced
²⁄₃ cup dry white wine
1 fresh parsley sprig
a pinch of sugar
1 tablespoon chopped
  fresh oregano
4 cups pappardelle or lasagnette
salt and freshly ground
  black pepper
freshly grated Parmesan cheese,
  to serve
fresh basil, to garnish

1 Peel the tomatoes, chop them roughly and put them in a pan. Add the onion, carrot, celery, wine, parsley sprig and sugar, and mix well. Bring to a boil, then lower the heat and simmer, half-covered, for 45 minutes, until very thick, stirring occasionally.

2 Remove and discard the parsley sprig. Transfer the tomato sauce to a blender or food processor and process until smooth, then return it to the clean pan. Stir in the oregano, season to taste with salt and pepper, and heat through gently.

3 Meanwhile, bring a large pan of lightly salted water to a boil and cook the pasta until it is *al dente*.

4 Drain the pasta thoroughly and return it to the clean pan. Add the sauce and toss to mix. Serve in warmed bowls, with grated Parmesan cheese, garnished with basil.

> **Cook's Tips**
> • Fresh Italian plum tomatoes are best for this sauce, especially if they have been home grown.
> • The sauce can be puréed by rubbing it through a fine strainer with the back of a wooden spoon.

Lasagnette with Tomato & Red Wine Sauce

A classic sauce that is simply delicious served with curly pasta. It needs no extra accompaniments.

Serves 4

1 tablespoon olive oil
1 onion, chopped
2 tablespoons tomato paste
1 teaspoon mild paprika
2 14-ounce cans
  chopped tomatoes
pinch of drained oregano
1¼ cups dry red wine
large pinch of sugar
12 ounces dried lasagnette or
  other long pasta
salt and freshly ground
  black pepper
chopped fresh flat-leaf parsley,
  to garnish
Parmesan cheese shavings,
  to serve (optional)

1 Heat the oil in a large, heavy frying pan. Add the onion and sauté over low heat, stirring occasionally, for 10 minutes, until softened. Stir in the tomato paste and paprika, and cook for 3 minutes.

2 Add the tomatoes, oregano, wine and sugar, and season with salt and pepper to taste. Bring to a boil, lower the heat and simmer for 20 minutes, until the sauce has reduced and thickened, stirring occasionally.

3 Meanwhile, bring a large pan of lightly salted water to a boil and cook the pasta until it is *al dente*.

4 Drain the pasta, return to the clean pan and toss with the tomato sauce. Serve in warmed bowls, garnished with chopped parsley and with Parmesan shavings sprinkled on top, if using.

Whole-wheat Pasta with Caraway Cabbage

Crunchy cabbage and Brussels sprouts are perfect partners for pasta in this healthy dish. Caraway seeds and cabbage are a classic combination. Not only do their flavors complement each other, but caraway is also an aid to digestion and reduces the odor of cabbage when it is cooking.

Serves 6

3 onions, roughly chopped
1²⁄₃ cups vegetable stock
12 ounces round white cabbage, roughly chopped
12 ounces Brussels sprouts, trimmed and halved
2 teaspoons caraway seeds
1 tablespoon chopped fresh dill
1³⁄₄ cups fresh or dried whole-wheat spirali
salt and freshly ground black pepper
fresh dill sprigs, to garnish

1 Put the onions in a large saucepan and add half the stock. Bring to a boil, cover and cook over low heat for about 10 minutes, stirring often, until the onion has softened and most of the liquid has been absorbed.

2 Add the cabbage and Brussels sprouts, and cook over high heat, stirring, for 2–3 minutes, then stir in the caraway seeds and chopped dill.

3 Pour in the remaining vegetable stock, and season with salt and pepper to taste. Cover and simmer over low heat for about 10 minutes, until the cabbage and Brussels sprouts are crisp-tender.

4 Meanwhile, bring a large pan of lightly salted water to a boil and cook the pasta until *al dente.*

5 Drain the pasta, put it in a bowl and add the cabbage mixture. Toss lightly, adjust the seasoning and serve immediately, garnished with dill sprigs.

Tagliatelle & Vegetable Ribbons

Zucchini and carrots are cut into thin, delicate ribbons so that when they are cooked and tossed with tagliatelle they look like colored pasta.

Serves 4

2 large zucchini
2 large carrots
9 ounces fresh egg tagliatelle
1 tablespoon extra virgin olive oil
flesh of 3 roasted garlic cloves, plus extra roasted garlic cloves, to serve (optional)
salt and freshly ground black pepper

1 With a vegetable peeler, cut the zucchini and carrots into long thin ribbons. Bring a large pan of lightly salted water to a boil and add the zucchini and carrot ribbons. Boil for 30 seconds, then lift out the vegetable ribbons with a slotted spoon and set them aside.

2 Add the tagliatelle to the boiling water and cook until it is *al dente.*

3 Drain the pasta and return it to the pan. Add the vegetable ribbons, oil and garlic, and season with salt and pepper to taste. Toss over medium to high heat until well mixed. Serve immediately, with extra roasted garlic, if desired.

Cook's Tip
Roasted garlic has a surprisingly mild and sweet flavor. To roast garlic, put a whole head of garlic on a lightly oiled baking sheet and drizzle a little extra olive oil on it. Place in a preheated 350°F oven and roast for 30–45 minutes. Remove the garlic from the oven and set it aside. When cool enough to handle, dig out the flesh from the cloves with the point of a knife, or simply squeeze the soft flesh from the individual cloves with your fingers. Individual cloves can be roasted in the same way; brushed with a little olive oil and cooked for about 20 minutes.

Fettuccine with Broccoli & Garlic

In this recipe, broccoli is mashed with wine and Parmesan to make a tasty coating sauce.

Serves 4
3–4 garlic cloves, crushed
2 1/2 cups broccoli florets
2/3 cup vegetable stock
1/4 cup white wine
2 tablespoons chopped fresh basil
1/4 cup freshly grated
   Parmesan cheese
12 ounces fresh or dried
   fettuccine or tagliatelle
salt and freshly ground
   black pepper
fresh basil leaves, to garnish

1 Put the garlic, broccoli and stock into a large saucepan. Bring to a boil over medium heat and cook for 5 minutes or until the broccoli is tender, stirring occasionally.

2 Mash with a fork or potato masher until the broccoli is roughly chopped. Stir in the white wine, chopped basil and Parmesan. Season to taste with salt and pepper, and leave over low heat while you cook the pasta.

3 Bring a large pan of lightly salted water to a boil and cook the fettuccine or tagliatelle until *al dente*.

4 Drain the pasta well and return to the pan. Pour on half the broccoli sauce and toss gently. Divide among warmed plates, top with the remaining broccoli sauce, garnish with the basil leaves and serve immediately.

Cook's Tip
When buying broccoli, look for stems that are neither dry and wrinkled nor woody, with tightly packed, dark green flowerheads. There should be no sign of yellowing. It is best eaten on the day of purchase and cannot be kept, even in a cool dark place, for more than a couple of days without the flowerheads turning yellow.

Tagliatelle with Broccoli & Spinach

This is an excellent vegetarian dinner dish. It is nutritious and filling and needs no accompaniment.

Serves 4
2 heads of broccoli
1 pound fresh spinach leaves,
   stems removed
freshly grated nutmeg
1 pound fresh or dried
   egg tagliatelle
1 tablespoon extra virgin olive oil
juice of 1/2 lemon
salt and freshly ground
   black pepper
freshly grated Parmesan cheese,
   to serve (optional)

1 Put the broccoli in the basket of a steamer, cover and steam over boiling water for 10 minutes.

2 Add the spinach to the broccoli, cover and steam for 4–5 minutes or until both the vegetables are tender. Toward the end of the cooking time, sprinkle them with freshly grated nutmeg, and season with salt and pepper to taste. Transfer the vegetables to a colander.

3 Add water to the steamer, as well as salt. Bring to a boil, then cook the pasta until *al dente*. Meanwhile, chop the broccoli and spinach.

4 Drain the pasta. Heat the oil in the pasta pan, add the pasta and chopped vegetables, and toss over medium heat until evenly mixed. Sprinkle in some of the lemon juice and plenty of black pepper, then taste and add more lemon juice, salt and nutmeg, if desired. Serve immediately, sprinkled with freshly grated Parmesan, if using, and black pepper.

Variations
• *To add both texture and protein, garnish the finished dish with 1/4 cup toasted pine nuts.*
• *Add a sprinkling of dried, crushed red chiles with the black pepper in step 4.*

Torchiette with Tossed Vegetables

Cooking the pasta in water flavored by the vegetables gives it a fresh taste.

Serves 4

8 ounces thin asparagus spears, trimmed and cut in half
1 cup snow peas, trimmed
⅔ cup baby corn
8 ounces whole baby carrots, trimmed
1 small red bell pepper, seeded and chopped
8 scallions, sliced
2 cups dried torchiette or other pasta shapes
⅔ cup low-fat cottage cheese
⅔ cup low-fat plain yogurt
1 tablespoon lemon juice
1 tablespoon chopped fresh parsley
1 tablespoon snipped chives
skim milk (optional)
salt and freshly ground black pepper

1 Bring a large pan of lightly salted water to a boil. Add the asparagus spears and cook for 2 minutes.

2 Add the snow peas and cook for 2 more minutes. Using a slotted spoon, transfer the vegetables to a colander, rinse them under cold water, drain and set aside.

3 Bring the water in the pan back to a boil, add the corn, carrots, red pepper and scallions, and cook until tender. Lift out with a slotted spoon. Drain in a colander, then rinse and drain again.

4 Bring the water back to a boil and add the pasta. Cook it until it is *al dente*.

5 Meanwhile, put the cottage cheese, yogurt, lemon juice, parsley and chives into a food processor or blender and process until smooth. Thin the sauce with skim milk, if necessary, and season to taste with salt and pepper.

6 Drain the pasta, return it to the clean pan, and add the vegetables and cottage cheese sauce. Toss lightly and serve immediately in warmed bowls.

Pasta with Tomato Sauce & Roasted Vegetables

This scrumptious dish also tastes good cold, and is great picnic fare.

Serves 4

1 eggplant
2 zucchini
1 large onion
2 bell peppers, preferably red or yellow, seeded
1 pound plum tomatoes
2–3 garlic cloves, roughly chopped
2 tablespoons olive oil
1¼ cups passata
8 black olives, halved and pitted (optional)
3 cups dried pasta shapes, such as rigatoni or penne
salt and freshly ground black pepper
¼ cup shredded fresh basil and four sprigs basil leaves, to garnish

1 Preheat the oven to 475°F. Cut the eggplant, zucchini, onion, peppers and tomatoes into large chunks. Discard the tomato seeds.

2 Spread out the vegetables in a large roasting pan. Sprinkle the garlic and oil onto the vegetables, and stir and turn to mix evenly. Season to taste with salt and pepper.

3 Roast the vegetables for 30 minutes or until they are soft and have begun to char around the edges. Stir halfway through the cooking time.

4 Scrape the vegetable mixture into a pan. Stir in the passata and olives, if using, and heat gently.

5 Bring a large pan of lightly salted water to a boil and cook the pasta until it is *al dente*.

6 Drain the pasta and return it to the clean pan. Add the sauce and toss to mix well. Serve immediately in a warmed bowl, sprinkled with the shredded basil and garnished with a basil sprig.

Pasta with Low-fat Pesto Sauce

Unlike traditional pesto, which is made with olive oil, this simple sauce is relatively low in fat but still full of flavor.

Serves 4

2 cups dried pasta shapes, such as fusilli or farfalle
1 cup fresh basil leaves
½ cup fresh parsley sprigs
1 garlic clove, crushed
¼ cup pine nuts
½ cup low-fat cottage cheese or very low-fat fromage frais
2 tablespoons freshly grated Parmesan cheese
salt and freshly ground black pepper
few sprigs of fresh basil, to garnish

1 Bring a large pan of lightly salted water to a boil and cook the pasta until *al dente*.

2 Meanwhile, put half the basil and half the parsley into a food processor or blender. Add the garlic, pine nuts and cottage cheese or fromage frais, and process until smooth.

3 Add the remaining basil and parsley, with the Parmesan, and season with salt and pepper to taste. Process until the herbs are finely chopped.

4 Toss the pasta with the pesto and serve immediately on warmed plates, garnished with fresh basil sprigs.

Cook's Tip
Fromage frais is a kind of cheese made from skim pasteurized cow's milk. Sometimes, it is enriched with cream to give it a firmer texture. However, this also gives it a higher fat content of about eight percent. Look for the softer type that is labeled "virtually fat-free," which has zero fat, or the slightly firmer low-fat fromage frais, which contains some fat. Make sure that you do not buy sweetened fromage frais which contains added sugar.

Farfalle with Bell Pepper Sauce

This healthy vegetarian dish is packed with vitamin C and full of flavor.

Serves 4

4 bell peppers, preferably mixed colors, halved and seeded
3 plum tomatoes, peeled and chopped
1 red onion, thinly sliced
1 garlic clove, thinly sliced
3 cups dried farfalle or other shapes
salt and freshly ground black pepper
2 tablespoons grated Parmesan cheese, to garnish (optional)

1 Preheat the broiler. Place the peppers, cut-side down, in a broiler pan and place under high heat until the skins have blistered and begun to char. Put them in a bowl and cover with several layers of paper towels. Set aside for 10–15 minutes.

2 Meanwhile, place the chopped tomatoes, onion and garlic in a heavy pan over low heat. Bring to the simmering point, cover and cook gently, stirring occasionally, for 8–10 minutes, until the onion is tender and the sauce has thickened.

3 Peel the skin from the peppers and slice the flesh thinly. Stir them into the tomato sauce, heat gently, and season with salt and pepper to taste. Leave the pan over low heat while you cook the pasta.

4 Bring a large pan of lightly salted water to a boil and cook the pasta until *al dente*.

5 Drain the pasta well and transfer to four warmed bowls. Top with the pepper sauce and serve, sprinkled with Parmesan cheese, if using.

Cook's Tip
Broiling the peppers not only makes them easy to peel, it also imparts a delicious flavor to the flesh, making it sweeter and less acerbic than when it is raw.

Tagliatelle with Sun-dried Tomatoes

Choose plain sun-dried tomatoes for this sauce, instead of those preserved in oil, as they would increase the fat content.

Serves 4
1 garlic clove, crushed
1 celery stalk, finely sliced
2 cups sun-dried tomatoes, finely chopped
6 tablespoons red wine
8 plum tomatoes
12 ounces dried tagliatelle
salt and freshly ground black pepper

1 Put the garlic, celery, sun-dried tomatoes and wine into a large saucepan. Cook over low heat, stirring occasionally, for 15 minutes.

2 Meanwhile, plunge the plum tomatoes into a saucepan of boiling water for 1 minute, then into cold water. Slip off their skins. Cut the tomatoes in half, scoop out the seeds and roughly chop the flesh.

3 Stir the plum tomatoes into the sun-dried tomato mixture, and season to taste with salt and pepper. Set the pan over low heat while you cook the pasta.

4 Bring a large pan of lightly salted water to a boil and cook the tagliatelle until it is *al dente*.

5. Drain the pasta well and return to the clean pan. Add half the tomato sauce and toss thoroughly to coat. Divide among warmed individual plates and top with the remaining sauce. Serve immediately.

Cook's Tip
This dish looks particularly attractive made with a mixture of plain, spinach-flavored and tomato-flavored tagliatelle. It is also delicious with whole-wheat pasta.

Ratatouille Penne

Marinated tofu adds interest to a popular vegetarian dish.

Serves 6
1 small eggplant
2 zucchini, thickly sliced
7 ounces firm tofu, cubed
3 tablespoons dark soy sauce
1 garlic clove, crushed
4 teaspoons sesame seeds
1 small red bell pepper, seeded and sliced
1 onion, finely chopped
1–2 garlic cloves, crushed
⅔ cup vegetable stock
3 firm ripe tomatoes, peeled, seeded and quartered
1 tablespoon chopped mixed fresh herbs
2 cups dried penne
salt and freshly ground black pepper

1 Cut the eggplant into 1-inch cubes. Put these into a colander with the zucchini, sprinkle with salt and set over the sink to drain for 30 minutes.

2 Put the tofu in a bowl and add the soy sauce, garlic and half the sesame seeds. Stir, cover and marinate for 30 minutes.

3 Put the pepper, onion, garlic and stock into a pan. Bring to a boil, cover and cook for 5 minutes, until the vegetables are tender. Remove the lid and boil until the stock has evaporated.

4 Rinse the eggplant and zucchini, drain and add to the pan, with the tomatoes and herbs. Cook for 10–12 minutes, until the eggplant and zucchini are tender, adding a little water if the mixture becomes too dry. Season to taste.

5 Meanwhile, bring a large pan of lightly salted water to a boil and cook the pasta until it is *al dente*. Drain thoroughly, return to the clean pan, and add the vegetable mixture and marinated tofu, with any liquid left in the bowl. Toss lightly, then put into a heated serving bowl and keep hot.

6 Spread out the remaining sesame seeds in a nonstick frying pan and quickly dry-fry them until golden. Sprinkle them onto the pasta dish and serve.

Pasta with Roasted Bell Pepper & Tomato Sauce

Add other vegetables, such as green beans, zucchini or even chickpeas, to make this delicious sauce even more substantial.

Serves 4
2 medium bell red peppers
2 medium bell yellow peppers
1 fresh red chile, seeded
1 tablespoon olive oil

1 medium onion, sliced
2 garlic cloves, crushed
14-ounce can chopped tomatoes
2 teaspoons balsamic vinegar
4 cups dried conchiglie or spirali
salt and freshly ground
   black pepper

1 Preheat the oven to 400°F. Spread out the peppers and chile in a roasting pan, and roast for 30 minutes or until softened and beginning to char. Remove the pan from the oven and cover with several layers of paper towels.

2 Meanwhile, heat the oil in a nonstick pan. Add the onion and garlic, and cook over low heat, stirring occasionally, for about 5 minutes, until soft and golden.

3 When the peppers and chile are cool enough to handle, rub off the skins. Cut them in half, remove the seeds and chop the flesh roughly.

4 Stir the chopped peppers and chile into the onion mixture, then add the tomatoes. Bring to a boil, lower the heat and simmer for 10–15 minutes, until slightly thickened and reduced. Stir in the vinegar, and season to taste with salt and freshly ground black pepper.

5 Meanwhile, bring a large pan of lightly salted water to a boil and cook the pasta until *al dente*.

6 Drain the pasta well and add it to the sauce. Toss thoroughly to mix, then serve immediately in warmed bowls.

Tagliatelle with "Hit-the-pan" Salsa

It is possible to make a hot, filling meal in just 15 minutes with this quick-cook salsa sauce.

Serves 2
4 ounces fresh tagliatelle
1 tablespoon extra virgin olive oil
1 garlic clove, crushed
4 scallions, sliced

1 green chile, halved, seeded
   and sliced
3 tomatoes, chopped
juice of 1 orange
2 tablespoons fresh
   parsley, chopped
salt and freshly ground
   black pepper
freshly grated Parmesan
   cheese (optional)

1 Bring a large pan of lightly salted water to a boil and cook the pasta until it is *al dente*. Drain and place in a large bowl. Add about 1 teaspoon of the oil and toss to coat. Season well with salt and pepper.

2 Preheat a wok, swirl in the remaining oil and, when it is hot, stir-fry the garlic, onions and chile for 1 minute. The pan should sizzle as they cook.

3 Add the tomatoes, orange juice and parsley. Season to taste with salt and pepper. Add the tagliatelle and toss over the heat until heated through. Divide among warmed individual plates and serve immediately with Parmesan cheese, if using.

Cook's Tip
When squeezing citrus fruits, make sure that they are at room temperature, as they will then yield more juice than they would straight from the refrigerator.

Variation
You could use any pasta shape for this recipe. The sauce would be particularly good with large rigatoni or linguini and would also work well with filled fresh pasta, such as ravioli or tortellini.

Tagliatelle with Pea Sauce, Asparagus & Fava Beans

When you're tired of tomatoes, try this creamy pea sauce, which tastes great with a mixture of pasta and vegetables.

Serves 4

1 tablespoon olive oil
1 garlic clove, crushed
6 scallions, sliced
2 cups frozen
    peas, thawed
12 ounces fresh young
    asparagus, trimmed
2 tablespoons chopped fresh
    sage, plus extra leaves
    to garnish
finely grated zest of 2 lemons
1¾ cups vegetable stock or water
1½ cups frozen fava beans,
    thawed
1 pound fresh or dried tagliatelle
¼ cup low-fat plain yogurt

1 Heat the oil in a pan. Add the garlic and scallions, and cook over low heat for 2–3 minutes, until softened.

2 Add the peas and one-third of the asparagus, together with the sage, lemon zest and stock or water. Bring to a boil, lower the heat and simmer for 10 minutes, until tender.

3 Transfer to a blender or food processor and process until smooth, then scrape the mixture into a pan. Pop the fava beans out of their skins and add them to the pan.

4 Cut the remaining asparagus into 2-inch lengths, trimming off any tough fibrous stems. Bring a large pan of lightly salted water to a boil, add the asparagus and cook for 2 minutes. Lift out with a slotted spoon and add to the pan of sauce. Reheat gently, stirring occasionally, while you cook the pasta.

5 Let the water return to a boil and add the tagliatelle. Cook until *al dente.*

6 Drain the pasta and return it to the clean pan. Add the yogurt and toss lightly. Divide among warmed plates and top with the sauce. Garnish with the extra sage leaves and serve.

Chinese Ribbons

This is a colorful Chinese-style dish, easily prepared using pasta instead of Chinese noodles.

Serves 4

1 medium carrot
2 small zucchini
6 ounces string or other
    green beans
6 ounces baby corn
1 pound dried ribbon pasta,
    such as tagliatelle
1 teaspoon sesame oil
1 tablespoon corn oil
salt
½-inch piece fresh ginger root,
    peeled and finely chopped
2 garlic cloves, finely chopped
6 tablespoons yellow bean sauce
6 scallions, sliced into
    1-inch lengths
2 tablespoons dry sherry
1 teaspoon sesame seeds

1 Slice the carrot and zucchini diagonally into chunks. Slice the beans diagonally. Cut the baby corn diagonally in half.

2 Bring a large pan of lightly salted water to a boil and cook the pasta until it is *al dente.*

3 Drain the pasta well, return to the clean pan and add the sesame oil. Toss to coat.

4 Preheat a wok, then swirl in the corn oil. When it is hot, add the ginger and garlic, and stir-fry over medium heat for 30 seconds, then add the carrots, beans, zucchini and corn, and stir-fry for 3–4 minutes.

5 Stir in the yellow bean sauce. Stir-fry for 2 minutes, add the scallions, sherry and pasta. Toss over the heat until piping hot. Divide among warmed bowls and serve immediately, sprinkled with sesame seeds.

Cook's Tip
Sesame oil has a strong nutty flavor and a distinctive aroma. It is generally used as a flavoring, rather than as a cooking oil.

Low-fat Tagliatelle with Mushrooms

Mushrooms cooked in stock, with wine and soy sauce have a superb flavor, and make a very good topping for fresh pasta. In addition, they contain no fat and no cholesterol at all.

Serves 4
1 small onion, finely chopped
2 garlic clove, crushed
²⁄₃ cup vegetable stock
3 cups mixed fresh mushrooms,
    quartered if large
¹⁄₄ cup white wine
2 teaspoons tomato paste
1 tablespoon soy sauce
8 ounces fresh sun-dried tomato
    and herb tagliatelle
1 teaspoon chopped fresh thyme
2 tablespoons chopped
    fresh parsley
salt and freshly ground
    black pepper
shavings of Parmesan cheese,
    to serve (optional)

1 Put the onion and garlic into a pan with the stock. Cover and cook over medium heat for 10 minutes or until tender.

2 Add the mushrooms, wine, tomato paste and soy sauce. Cover and cook for 5 minutes, then remove the lid from the pan and boil until the liquid has reduced by half.

3 Bring a large pan of lightly salted water to a boil and cook the pasta until it is *al dente*.

4 Meanwhile, stir the chopped fresh herbs into the mushroom mixture, and season with salt and pepper to taste.

5 Drain the pasta thoroughly, return it to the clean pan and add the mushroom mixture. Toss lightly and serve in warmed bowls, with the Parmesan, if desired.

Cook's Tip
Use cultivated or wild mushrooms, such as field, chestnut, oyster and chanterelle, or a mixture.

Tagliatelle with Spinach Gnocchi

Celebrate the sensible way with this sophisticated dish that looks and tastes indulgent but is relatively low in fat.

Serves 4–6
1 pound dried tagliatelle,
    preferably mixed colors
shavings of Parmesan cheese,
    to garnish

For the spinach gnocchi
1 pound frozen chopped spinach
1 small onion, finely chopped
1 garlic clove, crushed
¹⁄₄ teaspoon freshly
    grated nutmeg
1³⁄₄ cups low-fat cottage cheese
1 cup dried white bread crumbs
all-purpose flour, for dusting
³⁄₄ cup semolina or flour

²⁄₃ cup freshly grated
    Parmesan cheese
3 egg whites

For the tomato sauce
1 onion, finely chopped
1 celery stalk, finely chopped
1 red bell pepper, seeded
    and diced
1 garlic clove, crushed
²⁄₃ cup vegetable stock
14-ounce can chopped tomatoes
1 tablespoon tomato paste
2 teaspoons sugar
1 teaspoon dried oregano
salt and freshly ground
    black pepper

1 First, make the tomato sauce. Put the chopped onion, celery, pepper and garlic into a nonstick pan. Add the stock, bring to a boil and cook over medium heat for 5 minutes or until the vegetables are tender.

2 Stir in the tomatoes, tomato paste, sugar and oregano. Season to taste with salt and pepper, and bring to a boil. Lower the heat and simmer, stirring occasionally, for 30 minutes, until thickened.

3 Meanwhile, make the gnocchi. Put the frozen spinach, onion and garlic into a pan, cover and cook over low heat until the spinach has thawed. Remove the lid and increase the heat to cook off any moisture. Season with salt, pepper and nutmeg to taste. Transfer the spinach mixture to a bowl and set aside to cool completely.

4 Add the cottage cheese, bread crumbs, semolina or flour, Parmesan and egg whites to the spinach mixture, and mix. Using two teaspoons, shape the mixture into about 24 ovals and place them on a lightly floured tray. Place in the refrigerator for 30 minutes.

5 Bring a large shallow pan of lightly salted water to a boil, then lower the heat to a gentle simmer. Add the gnocchi in batches. As soon as they rise to the surface, after about 5 minutes, remove them with a slotted spoon and drain them thoroughly. Keep the cooked gnocchi hot.

6 Bring another large pan of salted water to a boil and cook the pasta until *al dente*. Drain thoroughly. Transfer to warmed serving plates, top with the spinach gnocchi and spoon on the tomato sauce. Sprinkle on shavings of Parmesan cheese and serve immediately.

Eggplant & Mixed Vegetable Lasagne

Kind of like a combination of lasagne and moussaka, this low-fat dish is quite filling, so it needs no accompaniment other than a small side salad.

Serves 6–8
1 large onion, finely chopped
2 garlic cloves, crushed
2/3 cup vegetable stock
1 small eggplant, cubed
3 cups mushrooms, sliced
14-ounce can chopped tomatoes
2 tablespoons tomato paste
1/2 cup red wine
1/4 teaspoon ground ginger
1 teaspoon mixed dried herbs
2 tablespoons low-fat spread

1/4 cup all-purpose flour
1 1/4 cups skim milk
a large pinch of freshly
    grated nutmeg
10–12 fresh lasagne sheets,
    precooked if necessary
scant 1 cup low-fat
    cottage cheese
1 egg, beaten
1/4 cup grated reduced-fat
    Cheddar cheese
2 tablespoons freshly grated
    Parmesan cheese
salt and freshly ground
    black pepper

1 Put the onion and garlic into a heavy saucepan with the stock. Cover and cook over medium heat for about 10 minutes or until tender.

2 Add the eggplant cubes, sliced mushrooms, tomatoes, tomato paste, wine, ginger and herbs. Bring to a boil, cover and cook for 15–20 minutes. Remove the lid and cook over high heat to evaporate the liquid by half. Season to taste with salt and pepper.

3 Put the low-fat spread, flour, skim milk and nutmeg into a pan. Whisk together over medium heat until thickened and smooth. Season with salt and pepper to taste.

4 Preheat the oven to 400°F. Spoon about one-third of the vegetable mixture into the bottom of an ovenproof dish. Cover with a layer of lasagne and one-quarter of the sauce.

5 Make two more layers in the same way, then cover with the cottage cheese. Beat the egg into the remaining sauce and pour it on top.

6 Sprinkle with the Cheddar and Parmesan, and bake for 25–30 minutes or until the top is golden brown. Let stand for about 10 minutes before serving.

> **Variation**
> *Add some soaked porcini mushrooms to intensify the flavor.*

Spinach & Hazelnut Lasagne

Lasagne is one of those dishes that almost everyone seems to like, and there will be plenty of takers for this low-fat vegetarian version.

Serves 4
2 pounds fresh spinach leaves,
    stems removed
1 1/4 cups vegetable stock
1 medium onion, finely chopped
1 garlic clove, crushed
3/4 cup hazelnuts

2 tablespoons chopped fresh basil
6 fresh lasagne sheets, precooked
    if necessary
14-ounce can chopped tomatoes
scant 1 cup low-fat fromage frais
salt and freshly ground
    black pepper
chopped hazelnuts and chopped
    fresh parsley, to garnish

1 Preheat the oven to 400°F. Wash the spinach and place it in a pan with just the water that clings to the leaves. Cover the pan and cook the spinach over fairly high heat for 2 minutes, shaking the pan frequently, until it has wilted. Drain well.

2 Heat 2 tablespoons of the stock in a large pan, add the chopped onion and garlic, and simmer until soft. Stir in the spinach, hazelnuts and basil.

3 In a large ovenproof dish, layer the spinach, lasagne sheets and tomatoes, seasoning each layer well. Pour in the remaining stock. Spread the fromage frais on top.

4 Bake the lasagne for about 45 minutes or until the topping is golden brown. Serve hot, sprinkled with lines of chopped hazelnuts and chopped parsley.

> **Cook's Tip**
> *The hazelnuts will taste even better if they are toasted. Spread them in a broiler pan and broil them until golden. Put them into a clean dish towel and rub off the skins.*

Pappardelle & Provençal Sauce

The flavors of the south of France are captured in this simple dish.

Serves 4
2 small red onions, peeled
²⁄₃ cup vegetable stock
1–2 garlic cloves, crushed
¼ cup red wine
2 zucchini, cut into fingers
1 yellow bell pepper, seeded and sliced
14-ounce can chopped tomatoes

2 teaspoons chopped fresh thyme
1 teaspoon sugar
12 ounces fresh pappardelle
salt and freshly ground black pepper
fresh thyme and 6 pitted black olives, roughly chopped, to garnish

1 Cut each onion into eight wedges, leaving the root end intact to hold them together during cooking. Put into a pan with the stock and garlic. Bring to a boil, lower the heat, cover and simmer for 5 minutes, until tender.

2 Add the red wine, zucchini, yellow pepper, tomatoes, chopped thyme and sugar, and season with salt and pepper to taste. Bring to a boil and cook over low heat for 5–7 minutes, gently shaking the pan occasionally to coat all the vegetables with the sauce.

3 Meanwhile, bring a large pan of lightly salted water to a boil and cook the pasta until it is *al dente*.

4 Drain the pasta well, put it in a warmed serving dish and top with the vegetable mixture. Garnish with the fresh thyme and chopped black olives, and serve immediately.

> **Cook's Tip**
> *When making the sauce, do not overcook the vegetables, as the dish is much nicer if they have a slightly crunchy texture to contrast with the tender pasta.*

Sweet-and-Sour Peppers with Farfalle

This Moroccan-inspired recipe has unusual ingredients, but the combination of flavors works very well.

Serves 4–6
1 red bell pepper
1 yellow bell pepper
1 orange bell pepper
1 garlic clove, crushed
2 tablespoons drained bottled capers

2 tablespoons raisins
1 teaspoon whole-grain mustard
grated zest and juice of 1 lime
1 teaspoon honey
2 tablespoons chopped cilantro
2 cups dried farfalle
salt and freshly ground black pepper
shavings of Parmesan cheese, to serve (optional)

1 Cut the peppers into quarters, at the same time removing the stems and seeds. Bring a large pan of water to a boil. Add the peppers and cook over medium heat for 10–15 minutes, until tender.

2 Drain, rinse under cold water and drain again. Peel off the skin and cut the flesh lengthwise into strips.

3 Put the garlic, capers, raisins, mustard, lime zest and juice, honey and cilantro into a bowl and whisk together. Season with salt and pepper to taste.

4 Bring a large pan of lightly salted water to a boil and cook the pasta until it is *al dente*.

5 Drain the pasta thoroughly, return it to the clean pan and add the reserved peppers and dressing. Toss over low heat for 1–2 minutes, then put in warmed serving bowls. Serve with a few shavings of Parmesan cheese, if using.

Spinach Ravioli Crescents

Impress your guests with these pretty pasta crescents filled with vegetables and cottage cheese.

Serves 4–6

1 bunch of scallions, finely chopped
1 carrot, coarsely grated
2 garlic cloves, crushed
scant 1 cup low-fat cottage cheese
1 tablespoon chopped fresh dill, plus extra to garnish
1/3 cup freshly grated Parmesan cheese
6 halves sun-dried tomatoes, finely chopped
1 batch of Basic Pasta Dough, flavored with spinach
beaten egg white, for brushing
all-purpose flour, for dusting
salt and freshly ground black pepper

1 Put the scallions, carrot, garlic and cottage cheese into a bowl. Add the chopped dill and Parmesan, then stir in two-thirds of the chopped sun-dried tomatoes. Season to taste with salt and pepper, and set aside.

2 Roll the spinach pasta into thin sheets and cut it into 3-inch rounds with a fluted ravioli or pastry cutter.

3 Place a spoon of filling in the center of each pasta round. Brush the edges with egg white, then fold each round in half to make crescents. Press the edges together to seal. Transfer to a floured dish towel to rest for 1 hour before cooking.

4 Bring a large pan of lightly salted water to a boil and cook the crescents in batches until they are just tender. Drain well.

5 Place the crescents on warmed serving plates and sprinkle on the remaining sun-dried tomatoes. Garnish with the extra chopped dill. Serve immediately.

> **Cook's Tip**
> *Spinach-flavored pasta not only looks pretty and complements the other ingredients, but it also seals better than plain pasta.*

Vegetarian Cannelloni

Cannelloni is great for entertaining, as it can be prepared in advance and popped into the oven when guests arrive.

Serves 4–6

1 onion, finely chopped
2 garlic cloves, crushed
2 carrots, coarsely grated
2 celery stalks, finely chopped
2/3 cup vegetable stock
1/2 cup red lentils
14-ounce can chopped tomatoes
2 tablespoons tomato paste
1/2 teaspoon ground ginger
1 teaspoon chopped fresh thyme
1 teaspoon chopped fresh rosemary
3 tablespoons low-fat spread
1/3 cup all-purpose flour
2 1/2 cups skim milk
1 bay leaf
a large pinch of freshly grated nutmeg
16–18 cannelloni tubes
1/4 cup grated reduced-fat Cheddar cheese
1/3 cup freshly grated Parmesan cheese
1/2 cup fresh white bread crumbs
salt and freshly ground black pepper
flat-leaf parsley, to garnish

1 Put the onion, garlic, carrots, celery and half the stock into a saucepan, cover and cook for 10 minutes, until tender. Add the lentils, tomatoes, tomato paste, ginger, thyme and rosemary. Stir in the remaining stock. Bring to a boil, lower the heat, cover and simmer for 20 minutes. Remove the lid and cook for about 10 minutes, until thick. Let cool.

2 Put the low-fat spread, flour, milk and bay leaf into a pan, and whisk over medium heat until thick and smooth. Season with salt, pepper and nutmeg. Discard the bay leaf.

3 Preheat the oven to 350°F. Spoon the lentil filling into the cannelloni. Spoon half the white sauce into the bottom of an ovenproof dish. Arrange the cannelloni in a single layer on top and spoon on the remaining sauce to cover.

4 Mix the cheeses and bread crumbs, then sprinkle on the cannelloni. Bake for 30–40 minutes. Garnish and serve.

Spaghetti with Mixed Bean Chili

Chickpeas and three different types of bean make this a hearty dish, ideal for coming home to after a long walk on a winter's day.

Serves 6

1 onion, finely chopped
1–2 garlic cloves, crushed
1 large fresh green chile, seeded
  and chopped
²/₃ cup vegetable stock
14-ounce can chopped tomatoes
2 tablespoons tomato paste
¹/₂ cup red wine
1 teaspoon dried oregano
7 ounces green beans, sliced
14-ounce can red kidney
  beans, drained
14-ounce can cannellini
  beans, drained
14-ounce can chickpeas, drained
1 pound dried spaghetti
salt and freshly ground
  black pepper

1 Put the chopped onion, garlic and chile into a nonstick pan and pour in the stock. Bring to a boil and cook over medium heat for 10 minutes, until the onion is tender.

2 Stir in the tomatoes, tomato paste, wine and oregano, and season with salt and pepper to taste. Bring to a boil, lower the heat, cover and simmer the sauce for 20 minutes.

3 Cook the beans in boiling, salted water for about 5–6 minutes, until tender. Drain thoroughly.

4 Add all the beans and the chickpeas to the sauce, and simmer for another 10 minutes. Meanwhile, bring a large pan of lightly salted water to a boil and cook the spaghetti until *al dente*. Drain thoroughly. Transfer to a serving dish and top with the chile. Serve immediately.

> **Cook's Tip**
> Use a package of chili seasoning mix instead of the fresh chile, if desired. Simply stir it into the sauce with the tomatoes.

Stir-fried Noodles with Bean Sprouts

A classic Chinese noodle recipe that is a perfect side dish.

Serves 4

6 ounces dried egg noodles
1 tablespoon vegetable oil
1 garlic clove, finely chopped
1 small onion, halved and sliced
4 cups bean sprouts
1 small red bell pepper, seeded
  and cut into strips
1 small green bell pepper, seeded
  and cut into strips
¹/₂ teaspoon salt
¹/₄ teaspoon freshly ground
  white pepper
2 tablespoons light soy sauce

1 Bring a pan of lightly salted water to a boil and cook the noodles until they are just tender, checking the package for information on timing. Drain, rinse under cold water and drain well again.

2 Preheat a wok and swirl in the oil. When it is hot, add the garlic, stir briefly, then add the onion slices. Stir-fry for 1 minute over medium heat, then add the bean sprouts and peppers, and stir-fry for 2–3 minutes.

3 Stir in the drained noodles and toss over the heat, using two spatulas or wooden spoons, for 2–3 minutes or until the ingredients are well mixed and have heated through.

4 Add the salt, pepper and soy sauce, and stir thoroughly before serving the noodle mixture in warmed bowls.

> **Cook's Tip**
> White pepper comes from peppercorns that have ripened fully, unlike green or black peppercorns. The skin and outer flesh have been removed. White pepper is hot but not so aromatic as black pepper.

Five-spice Vegetable Noodles

Spicy, with delicious warmth from the chile, ginger, cinnamon and other spices, this is exactly the right dish to serve for dinner on a cold winter's evening.

Serves 2–3
8 ounces dried egg noodles
2 carrots
1 celery stalk
1 small fennel bulb
1 tablespoon vegetable oil
2 zucchini, halved and sliced
1 fresh red chile, seeded and chopped, plus sliced red chile to garnish (optional)
1-inch piece fresh ginger root, grated
1 garlic clove, crushed
1½ teaspoons Chinese five-spice powder
½ teaspoon ground cinnamon
4 scallions, sliced
¼ cup warm water

1 Bring a large pan of lightly salted water to a boil and cook the noodles briefly until they are just tender, checking the package for information on timing. Drain, rinse under cold water and drain again.

2 Cut the carrots and celery into julienne. Cut the fennel bulb in half and cut out the hard core. Cut the flesh into slices, then into julienne.

3 Preheat a wok and swirl in the oil. When it is hot, add the carrots, celery, fennel, zucchini and chile, and stir-fry over medium heat for 7–8 minutes.

4 Add the ginger and garlic, and stir-fry for 2 minutes, then stir in the Chinese five-spice powder and cinnamon, and stir-fry for 1 minute more.

5 Add the scallions and stir-fry for 1 minute. Moisten with the warm water and cook for 1 more minute.

6 Add the noodles, and toss and stir over the heat until well mixed and heated through. Divide the noodles among warmed individual bowls, garnish with sliced fresh red chile, if desired, and serve immediately.

Tofu Stir-fry with Egg Noodles

The sauce for this stir-fry is absolutely delicious, and the marinated tofu adds both substance and an interesting contrast in texture.

Serves 4
8 ounces firm smoked tofu
3 tablespoons dark soy sauce
2 tablespoons red vermouth
8 ounces medium dried egg noodles
2 teaspoons honey
2 teaspoons cornstarch
3 leeks, thinly sliced
1-inch piece fresh ginger root, finely grated
1–2 fresh red chiles, seeded and sliced into rings
1 small red bell pepper, seeded and thinly sliced
⅔ cup vegetable stock
salt and freshly ground black pepper

1 Cut the tofu into ¾-inch cubes. Put it into a bowl with the soy sauce and vermouth. Toss well to coat, then set aside to marinate for 30 minutes.

2 Bring a large pan of lightly salted water to a boil and cook the noodles briefly until they are just tender. Drain, rinse under cold water and drain again.

3 Lift the tofu from the marinade. Reserve the marinade and fry the tofu quickly in a nonstick frying pan until lightly golden brown on all sides. Remove from heat. Mix the honey and cornstarch into the marinade and set it aside.

4 Put the leeks, ginger, chile, pepper and stock into a large pan. Bring to a boil and cook over high heat for 2–3 minutes, until the vegetables are crisp-tender.

5 Add the reserved marinade to the vegetable mixture and cook over high heat, stirring constantly, until it thickens. Add the noodles and tofu, and toss over the heat until both have heated through. Season to taste with salt and pepper.

6 Divide the stir-fry and noodles among warmed individual plates and serve immediately.

Noodles Primavera

As tasty as it is colorful, this is a substantial dish destined to become a favorite with the whole family.

Serves 4

8 ounces dried broad
   rice noodles
scant 1 cup broccoli florets
1 carrot, thinly sliced lengthwise
8 ounces asparagus, trimmed and
   cut into 2-inch lengths
1 red or yellow bell pepper,
   seeded and cut into strips
2 ounces baby corn

½ cup sugar snap peas, trimmed
2 tablespoons vegetable oil
1 tablespoon chopped
   fresh ginger root
2 garlic cloves, chopped
2 scallions, finely chopped
1 pound tomatoes, chopped
1 bunch of arugula leaves
soy sauce, to taste
salt and freshly ground
   black pepper

1 Soak the noodles in hot water for about 30 minutes, until soft. Drain.

2 Bring a large pan of lightly salted water to a boil and blanch the broccoli florets for 1 minute. Lift out with a slotted spoon, refresh under cold water, drain and set aside.

3 Repeat this process in turn with the carrot, asparagus, red or yellow pepper, baby corn and sugar snap peas, keeping all the vegetables separate.

4 Preheat a wok, add the oil and swirl it around. Add the ginger, garlic and scallions, and stir-fry for 30 seconds over medium heat. Then add the tomatoes and stir-fry for 2–3 minutes.

5 Add the noodles to the wok and toss over the heat for 3 minutes to heat through. Toss in the blanched vegetables and arugula leaves. Season with soy sauce, salt and pepper to taste, and cook, stirring and tossing constantly, until the vegetables are tender and the dish is piping hot. Transfer to a warmed serving bowl and serve immediately.

Asian Vegetable Noodles

Fresh shiitake mushrooms and sesame oil are authentic Asian ingredients in this tasty stir-fry, but it is Italian balsamic vinegar that gives it the edge.

Serves 6

1¼ pounds fine dried egg noodles
1 red onion

1½ cups fresh
   shiitake mushrooms
1 tablespoon vegetable oil
3 tablespoons dark soy sauce
1 tablespoon balsamic vinegar
2 teaspoons sugar
1 teaspoon salt
1 teaspoon sesame oil
celery leaves, to garnish

1 Bring a large saucepan of lightly salted water to a boil. Add the egg noodles and cook briefly until they are just tender. Drain thoroughly.

2 Thinly slice the red onion and the shiitake mushrooms. Preheat a wok, then add the vegetable oil and swirl it around. When the oil is hot, add the onion and mushrooms, and stir-fry for 2 minutes.

3 Add the noodles to the wok with the soy sauce, balsamic vinegar, sugar and salt. Toss them over the heat for 2–3 minutes, then add the sesame oil. Transfer to a warmed bowl and serve immediately, garnished with the celery leaves.

Cook's Tip
Shiitake mushrooms have a unique flavor and texture. Originating in the East, they are now widely cultivated in Europe and the United States. The caps are velvety and tan in color, sometimes with light veins or faint white spots. The stems are often quite tough and may need to be removed before cooking. Otherwise, simply wipe the mushrooms with paper towels. Do not wash them, otherwise they will absorb more moisture. There is also no need to peel them. Shiitake mushrooms should be cooked gently and briefly, as prolonged cooking tends to make them tough and unpalatable.

Spicy Vegetable Chow Mein

Ten minutes is all the time it takes to make this simply delicious snack.

Serves 3
8 ounces dried egg noodles
4 ounces green beans
2 tablespoons vegetable oil
2 garlic cloves, crushed
1 onion, chopped
1 small red bell pepper, seeded and chopped
1 small green bell pepper, seeded and chopped
1 celery stalk, finely chopped
½ teaspoon Chinese five-spice powder
1 vegetable bouillon cube, crumbled
½ teaspoon freshly ground black pepper
1 tablespoon soy sauce
salt

1 Bring a large pan of lightly salted water to a boil and cook the noodles briefly until they are just tender. Drain and spread out on a large plate to cool.

2 Blanch the beans in lightly salted boiling water for 1 minute, then remove and drain.

3 Preheat a wok. Swirl in the oil and stir-fry the beans, garlic, onion, peppers and celery, tossing them to mix.

4 Stir in the five-spice powder and crumble in the bouillon cube. Stir in the black pepper and cook for 3 minutes.

5 Stir in the noodles and soy sauce. Toss the mixture over the heat for 2–3 minutes, until the noodles have heated through and are coated in the sauce. Transfer to a warmed serving bowl and serve immediately.

Cook's Tip
Chinese five-spice powder is a mixture of star anise, pepper, fennel, cloves and cinnamon. It is available at supermarkets and Chinese food stores. When buying, make sure you have Chinese powder, as Indian five-spice powder is different.

Chow Mein with Cashews

It is the lemon sauce that makes this chow mein extra special.

Serves 4
8 ounces dried egg noodles
1 tablespoon vegetable oil
½ cup cashews
2 carrots, cut into matchsticks
3 celery stalks, cut into matchsticks
1 green bell pepper, seeded and cut into thin strips
4 cups bean sprouts
salt
2 tablespoons toasted sesame seeds, to garnish

For the lemon sauce
2 tablespoons light soy sauce
1 tablespoon dry sherry
⅔ cup vegetable stock
grated zest and juice of 2 lemons
1 tablespoon sugar
2 teaspoons cornstarch

1 Stir all the ingredients for the lemon sauce together in a bowl. Bring a large pan of lightly salted water to a boil and cook the noodles until they are just tender. Drain and spread out on a plate to dry.

2 Preheat a wok and swirl in the oil. Add the cashews, toss them quickly over high heat until golden, then remove them with a slotted spoon and drain on paper towels.

3 Add the carrots and celery to the wok, and stir-fry over medium heat for 4–5 minutes. Add the green pepper and bean sprouts, and stir-fry for 2–3 more minutes.

4 Using a slotted spoon or spider, lift the vegetables out of the wok and set them aside on a plate. Pour the lemon sauce mixture into the wok and cook, stirring constantly, for about 2 minutes, until it is thick.

5 Return the vegetables to the pan, add the noodles and toss over the heat until heated through.

6 Finally, add the cashews and toss them with the noodles and vegetables. Serve immediately on heated plates, with the toasted sesame seeds sprinkled on top.

Index